Other books by Susan Farewell:

MOBIL ROAD ATLAS AND TRIP PLANNING GUIDE
(published annually, Simon & Schuster)

NEW ENGLAND ROAD ATLAS
(1991, Simon & Schuster)

PACIFIC NORTHWEST ATLAS
(1992, Simon & Schuster)

Other Books in the Paragon House Writer's Series

HOW TO PREPARE YOUR MANUSCRIPT FOR A PUBLISHER
by David L. Carroll

A MANUAL OF WRITER'S TRICKS
by David L. Carroll

GHOSTWRITING: HOW TO GET INTO THE BUSINESS
by Eva Shaw

WRITING AND SELLING MAGAZINE ARTICLES
by Eva Shaw

FORMATTING YOUR SCREENPLAY
by Rick Reichman

WRITING EFFECTIVE SPEECHES
by Henry Ehrlich

HOW TO WRITE SCIENCE FICTION
by Matthew Costello

How to Make a Living as a Travel Writer

Susan Farewell

PARAGON HOUSE
New York

First edition, 1992

Published in the United States by

Paragon House Publishers
90 Fifth Avenue
New York, NY 10011

Library of Congress Cataloging-in-Publication Data

Farewell, Susan
How to make a living as a travel writer / Susan Farewell. — 1st ed.
p. cm. — (Paragon House writer's series)
ISBN 1-55778-538-4
1. Travel—Authorship. I. Title. II. Series.
G151.F37 1992
808'.06691—dc20 92-6843
CIP

Manufactured in the United States of America

1 3 5 7 9 10 8 6 4 2

Dedication

To my parents—Barbara and Russell Farewell—who taught me that to travel is to learn and to live, and that having a loving home to come back to makes it all possible.

Acknowledgments

I could probably fill a book this size if I were to mention everyone who has in some way supported, encouraged, or inspired me to become a freelance travel writer and to write this book. Two books, if I were to name everyone in tourism in countries around the world who has helped me along the way.

Instead, there are just a handful of people who deserve a special thanks for their time and support during the writing of this book: Joanne Farewell King, Mary Loncin, Audrey Liounis, and my agent—Susan Urstadt—who convinced me that it was time to get this book out of my head and on to paper.

Contents

Introduction

"So, what's your schedule like these days?" a travel writer friend of mine recently asked on the phone.

"Well, I leave for Iceland Friday and I'll be there for a week."

"Oh, Iceland—I love Iceland. Be sure to go to the restaurant Ooinsve in Reykjavik. Order the Arctic charr. When you get back, we'll have to get together, but after I get back from Barbados."

"You're going to Barbados? You've got to call my friend Margaret when you're down there. She knows everything there is to know about Barbados. In fact, I'm going there next month to update my book."

"Oh well, maybe I'll wait and go with you. (Pause as she looks at her calendar). No, actually, I can't. I'll be driving down the coast of Oregon for a story."

"Oregon. Lucky you. There's a wonderful inn in Newport . . ."

If a so-called "normal" person (or a "mortal" as my friend Tad refers to people who are not travel writers) heard this conversation, they'd think that surely those two people were wealthy braggarts trying to outdo one another. For travel writers, however, this is a fairly typical conversation.

Travel writing is one of the few professions where you not only travel but are under some obligation to actually enjoy the places you visit. In order to get your research done, you must eat in its restaurants, stay in some of its top hotels, visit its museums, its gardens, its archaeological sites—you name it. Still, few veteran travel writers will tell you they *get* to travel. In fact, the first question I'm asked when someone learns what I do for a living is "Does that mean you get to travel?" My immediate response is "Get to? *Have* to is more like it." As wonderful as travel can be, trying to juggle it with writing about it can be tremendously challenging. Somehow, even a trip to Fiji when you have three articles due can be an imposition.

The second question I am inevitably asked is "Can you actually make a living as a travel writer?" The good news is yes, indeed you can. The bad news is that it's hard. This is a profession that requires several aptitudes as well as skills, along with an inexhaustible passion for travel and a great deal of your time—if not all of it.

Perhaps the most important thing to keep in mind if you're considering becoming a travel writer is a firm grasp on reality. It's quite common for those with an incredible capacity for fantasy to gravitate to this field. As glamorous as the profession may sound, it's not just a matter of throwing a dart at a map and going wherever it sticks in. As with any other profession, it is a business and requires a great deal of planning and discipline. At the same time, it's an art and requires great creativity.

On the following pages, you'll not only find out how you can go about breaking into the business, but learn how to become successful at it as well.

Part One

ARE YOU CUT OUT TO BE A TRAVEL WRITER?

CHAPTER 1

The Mind of the Travel Writer

1.1 The Persona

Have you ever sat on a city park bench or in a train station and tried to figure out what everyone who walked by you did for a living? Clearly, some people are lawyers, some are secretaries, some are hairdressers. Okay, okay, okay. Not *every* profession is immediately identifiable.

Let's say, however, that you were sitting on the same bench, and somebody told you that out of twenty people that would walk by, five of them would be travel writers, and you would have to point out who they were. Like trying to find the name *Nina* in Hirschfeld's cartoons, this is not necessarily an easy task.

Not all travel writers are going to show up dressed in Banana Republic clothes with cameras dangling over their shoulders. In fact, few—if even any—will. Travel writers come in all sizes and shapes and ages. Attend a travel writer event and you will see everything from the model-like ingenue that writes for *Vogue* to the old curmudgeon who has been freelancing for newspapers since ship travel was the customary mode of transportation. Travel writers can be ex-lawyers, ex-photographers, someday-to-be editors-in-chief, someday-to-be piano teachers, or travel writers for life—you name it. It's a profession that attracts people who want to travel, and hopefully, those who know how to write. Travel writers are not necessarily intrepid, strong, spirited people. In fact, some of the world's most fragile looking people—and self-proclaimed "wimps"—have managed to do quite well in the business.

1.2 The Aptitudes and Traits

Whether or not you can survive as a travel writer will take time—and trial and error—to discover. However, there are many aptitudes and traits it helps to have in order to effectively run a travel writing business. Here are some of the most necessary:

1. *Independence*
   Travel writers work largely alone and must rely on their own resources.
2. *Creativity, innovativeness, resourcefulness*
   All three of these are necessary in order to develop story ideas and write well.
3. *Risk-taking*
   This is a business rife with risks. They run the gamut from not knowing whether you'll have a steady income to flying into politically unsteady countries.
4. *Flexibility*
   Travel writers are constantly putting personal plans on hold and juggling professional responsibilities.
5. *Motivation*
   Self-employed writers are responsible for motivating themselves.
6. *High Energy*
   Some full-time travel writers work as much as medical interns.

7. *Discipline*

   Travel writers can start work at 9 A.M., 3 P.M., or at 3 A.M. You're your own boss.

8. *Organization*

   Unfortunately, many travel writers suffer from incurable disorganization. It is a profession where paper can easily take over, where schedules can be hectic, and where being organized is a big plus.

9. *Optimism*

   This is not to say one must go around happy, joyous, and free all the time. It's important, however, that one have a healthy supply of hope and faith. Though pessimism can be a great motivator, it can also erode the spirit.

10. *Enthusiasm*

    Travel writers often have to write about the same people, places, and things over and over again. It can get boring.

11. *Perseverance*

    Sometimes, it's necessary to pursue an assignment over a great length of time before actually getting it. The writer must be patient and persevere.

12. *Decision-making*

    Travel writers have to make a lot of decisions. Passive personalities have a hard time in this business.

13. *Orientation to goals*

    To want to see your name in print, to want to write a book, to want to travel to every country in the Far East. It's important to have goals in this business. They give you direction.

14. *Orientation to people*

    Many people assume that writers live very isolated existences. Though this at times is true, travel writers generally spend a great deal of time with other people. These include fellow writers who they may travel with, various editors and publishers, public relations executives, and tourist industry officials.

15. *Competitiveness*
    For every magazine article that gets published, there are thousands that don't. A travel writer should have a competitive spirit, but at the same time a healthy respect for fellow writers.
16. *Confidence*
    It's of major importance that you are pleased with your writing style and ability. This not only shows in your work, but in your character as well.
17. *Leadership*
    This is especially necessary if you're going to oversee large projects where other writers, fact-checkers, researchers, and various other independent contractors are involved.
18. *Responsibility*
    You are responsible for what you write and how you run your business. It is imperative that you take these responsibilities seriously.

1.3 The Education

Do you have to study journalism? Do you have to be an English major? Do you have to get an advanced degree? Strangely enough, in order to become a travel writer, the answer to all three of these questions is no. I was a Greek Classics major in college. Other travel writers I know studied Political Science, Art History, Education—you name it.

Many people do not discover the travel writing profession until after they've completed college and sometimes, a law degree later, or perhaps a couple of career changes down the road.

Of course, if you grow up knowing you want to be a travel writer, it sure can help to take a lot of English courses along the way. But it also helps to diversify your background. For example, the Classics background was a wonderful foundation for me in that it took me over to Greece where I began writing about my travels. It also forced me to read and write a great deal. If you know you want to write about the United States or Europe, it certainly helps if you have an understanding of the area's history, geology, politics, etc. If you have a degree in architecture but have decided the field is too saturated, or for whatever reasons, have decided not to go ahead with it, you can write about travel from an architectural point of view. Just about any field of study can be applied to travel writing. In other words, no education is a wasted education for a travel writer.

There are a handful of skills you will need in order to support yourself as a travel writer. They include:

1. *Ability to write*
   Clearly, you must know how to write. This can take years of practice and many rejections.
2. *Computer literacy*
   If you're still using a typewriter or, perish the thought, writing articles longhand (don't laugh, the head writer of a leading soap opera writes out all the plots on legal pads), you won't be able to compete with the high-tech writers that are out there.

1.4 A Travel Writer Quiz

Are you cut out to be a travel writer? Circle the letter that best describes you.

1. You've missed your flight out of Cairo, the next several are booked, and the ticket agent says serenely, "Don't worry.

Allah willed this." Meanwhile, you have three more countries to "cover" in one week. You:

a) Scream irately at the ticket agent.
b) Head straight for the bar.
c) Secure a flight for the next day, go back into town and settle in for an obligation-free evening at your hotel.

2. You are terribly afraid of take-offs and landings, so you:

a) Drive, take trains, buses, or ships whenever possible.
b) Drink yourself into oblivion.
c) Bury yourself in a book or a conversation with the person sitting next to you during those times.

3. You're in Caracas, Venezuela. A new-found pilot friend invites you on a private sightseeing flight to Angel Falls. "Guaranteed to give you a close-up view," he says with a devilish smile. You:

a) Say thanks, but no thanks.
b) Take a rain check.
c) Accept with pleasure.

4. You're up against a deadline for a major article about skiing in Scandinavia when an editor calls and asks if you can give her a quick 1,000-word piece on Caribbean inns. You know both subjects very well. You:

a) Say no thanks, I'm too busy at the moment.
b) Say yes and miss your other deadline.
c) Ask for a bit more time from both editors.

5. You have to write a piece on a place you absolutely hated, for a magazine you never heard of before. You're in no mood to work on it, yet it is due in days. You:

a) Procrastinate till after the deadline and then ask for an extension.
b) Write it half-heartedly.
c) Talk yourself into getting something out of writing it.

6. You get a call asking if you could lecture on a subject you just wrote extensively about. You can't stand speaking in front of groups, so you:

a) Say no thank you.
b) Say yes, but change your mind later.
c) Say yes, definitively.

7. You have no work. You haven't had work for three months. You've taken loans against your CDs. You:

a) Try to find a "real job" at a magazine or book publishing company.
b) Spend your time bellyaching to everyone on the phone.
c) Keep networking, sending out proposals, and calling editors.

8. It's 3 A.M. You've been at your computer for so long, your eyes hurt, your back aches, you're feeling nauseous. Still, your article is due at noon the next day and the editor will not grant you an extension. You:

a) Continue working through the night.
b) Blow off the deadline.
c) Get a couple of hours rest before finishing up.

9. In ten years, you picture yourself:

a) You're not sure.
b) As a lawyer.
c) As a well-known author or journalist.

10. You've just received a call from an innkeeper. He is irate because you mentioned his inn on the same page as a group of seedy hotels in his town. How dare you associate him with such places. You:

    a) Tell him to go you know where.
    b) Cry.
    c) Tell him you admire his integrity and explain that most innkeepers are thrilled to get any kind of publicity.

11. An editor calls with an immediate project. There is no way you could free up to do it and he asks if you could recommend another writer. You:

    a) Lie. Pretend you can't think of any body.
    b) Recommend a writer you know is on the road.
    c) Give him a few names, but explain that you have never worked directly with them (unless you of course have, and in that case, can highly recommend them).

12. It's spring. You'd love to have some new clothes. The only problem is that prices are at their highest. You:

    a) Charge everything and worry about it later.
    b) Buy just one wonderful sweater to make you feel happy.
    c) Mix and match what you have and wait for the sales.

13. You write:

    a) Only checks.
    b) Only when you have to.
    c) Almost every day.

If you circled all A's and B's, you may have a difficult time supporting yourself as a travel writer. However, many of these traits evolve over time and through experience, so don't necessarily give up. If you circled mostly C's, you already have what it takes.

Part Two

DEVELOPING YOUR STYLE

CHAPTER 2

Learning the Basics On Your Own

2.1 Read As Much As You Can

One of the best ways to become a good travel writer is rather obvious: read a lot. Read in the bathtub, read while you eat (not the shredded wheat box), read on the subway, read while you sit in traffic, read before you go to sleep, read on the Stairmaster. And be selective about what you read. Read good fiction—both travel and non-travel. Read every travel magazine you can get your hands on. If not complete articles, at least read leads, headlines. If you're going to be traveling, read a novel that was set in that particular destination or written by one of the destination's local authors.

2.2 Do a Writing Workout

If you want to learn how to play tennis, you must play tennis. If you want to have a beautifully-toned body, you must work out regularly. Becoming a good travel writer is like absolutely everything else: You must work at it. To get started, set aside at least half an hour three days a week—or better yet, every day—to do travel writing exercises, just as you would jog or do aerobics.

Choose whichever medium you feel most comfortable with—a thin-lined legal pad and pencil (or pen), a typewriter, or a computer (for some of these exercises, you'll need a laptop). Choose instruments you physically like the feel of. If you prefer the touch of the computer keyboard to writing long hand, by all means use the computer. Doing travel writing exercises is a very disciplined task, so it's necessary to make yourself as comfortable as possible.

Once you get into a routine of practicing, you can create your own exercises, but here are some to get you started. Each day, record the date at the top of the page or screen and save everything you write.

1. *Expand Your Color Spectrum*

Wherever you happen to be, look out your window and describe the colors you see in as many new ways as possible. In a New England fall, the leaves are not just red, yellow, and orange. They may be yellow as taxi cabs or the color of bananas. The reds may be blood-red or a sports car-red. The oranges, like cooked lobsters or pumpkin pie. If you're on vacation in the Caribbean, do not—repeat, *do not*—write that "the water is turquoise." Think, think, think. Is it the color of pistachio ice cream, the color of aged copper? Is it clear as gin (how about clear as windows) or lapis lazuli blue? Is the sand merely white or does it look washed in bleach?

For each color you see, try to come up with at least three of your own adjectives that describe it to a T.

2. *Become a Human Tape Recorder*

Focus your attention on what it is you hear at this very moment. Jot down every sound—no thoughtful adjectives necessary unless they pop into mind.

For example: Let's imagine you are having a capuccino in a café. Here's what you might hear and jot down:

> A blender whirling away furiously, a young couple bickering in the corner, a dog barking incessantly outside the door, a waiter imitating a customer's lockjaw with co-workers behind the counter.

Or suppose you are in a residential city neighborhood. From your window, you might hear:

> A neighbor washing pots and pans. A window being pushed open. A scale being played on a piano. A plane overhead.

3. *Record What You Smell*

This exercise is exactly like #2 but record what you smell.

4. *Study your View*

Look out your kitchen window, or wherever you happen to be sitting, and examine your view. Try to find something in the view that you've been looking at for years, but haven't thought about. For example, maybe there is a stone wall, or part of one. Take the thought and run with it. Are there lots of stone walls in this area? Is this an old stone wall or a new stone wall? Try to picture who built it. Write a paragraph about what stone walls mean to you. Do they keep animals out and people in, or animals in and people out? Are they like bulging veins on the earth? Do they separate the landscape into neat little packages?

5. *Make Up Metaphors and Similes*

This is an exercise you can do while waiting in the grocery store line, while driving, while riding the subway, showering, what have you. Observe what's going on in you or around you and play with new ways to describe it. Jot them down as soon as you can. For example:

> I was sitting on the subway today and ideas starting *sprouting like popcorn* (or *sprouting like mushrooms after a rain*, or *sprouting like dandelions*) in my head.

> I saw a woman so distraught that she missed a bus, you would have thought it *drove off with her future.*

> The rain hit the window and *scattered like mercury.*

6. *Practice Writing Leads*

Find a travel story lead that's rather ho hum and rewrite it. Or start from scratch. Try to come up with the most clever lead you possibly can, but avoid being too cutesy or prosy.

7. *Review a Restaurant*

Whenever you have a meal out, write a review of the restaurant. Describe the menu, the dishes, the decor, the service, the view.

8. *Write a Travel Piece About a Place from Your Past*

Try to remember a place you went to as a child and write about it. What do you remember most? Try to recall as much detail as you possibly can. Keep it short, maybe a page or two.

2.3 Study Other Writers' Works

Have you ever started to read a travel article because it was about a destination you hoped to visit someday only to have stopped after a paragraph or two, torn it out, and stashed it away in a file? You were probably thinking along the "I'm too busy now, but I'll read it later" lines. I call these files the halfway house—halfway between your office and the trash can. They often end up forgotten about and tossed out years later.

On the other hand, have you ever started to read a travel piece about a destination you had no intention of going to, but found yourself putting off everything else until you'd devoured every word of it?

Good travel writing can be wonderfully compelling. It can also teach you a lot about how to develop your own style. Here are a handful of exercises you can do regarding other people's writings.

1. *Become a Lead Critic*

Make it an ongoing habit to read through leads of travel stories and rate them. If they leave you cold, give them a *1*. If they intrigue you, but sound a little overdone, give them a *3*. If they are wonderfully new and ingenious, give them a *10*.

2. *Play Editor*

For this exercise, have your newspaper travel section and a bossy red pen in hand. Pick an article—any article—and go through circling clichés and redundancies. Ask yourself whether the article convincingly creates a sense of place. If the title of the story isn't catchy enough, come up with another one (or several). If you find yourself totally bored by the second paragraph, write "yawn" in the margin. If the article rambles on too long, write "wordy." If information is missing, jot down questions you might have. If a fact is questionable, put a question mark beside it. Be ruthless.

3. *Become an Article Architect*

For some writers, ideas and words come easily, but building a story is enormously difficult. Where do you start? Where do you go? How do you wrap it up? How do you make smooth transitions? One exercise to help you build articles is to take a newspaper or magazine piece and cut out all the paragraphs individually, mix them up, and then arrange them so they make sense.

CHAPTER 3

Studying With Others

3.1 Writers' Workshops and Conferences

At various universities and writers' centers around the country, there are periodic workshops and conferences. These differ from place to place, but basically they offer writers opportunities to get feedback, suggestions, and advice about their work from successful, accomplished authors.

These can be enormously inspiring and informative. They can also be a good place to meet other writers, editors, and agents. Workshops can cover everything from "How to Write for Women's Magazines" to "How to Land a Book Agent." Not all offer travel writing workshops; inquire beforehand.

To find out about conferences and workshops that might be of interest to you, flip through a copy of *Poets & Writers Magazine* where many of them advertise. Another source is *The Guide to Writers Conferences* (Shaw Guides, Inc.) which includes information on hundreds of conferences, residencies, and retreats.

3.2 Classes

If you get pangs every fall to take a class and learn something new, it can't hurt to take a course to further your writing or editing skills. Contact your local universities and colleges about the various journalism, writing, and publishing courses they may offer.

Consider also taking other courses such as computer workshops to upgrade your skills or courses that have to do with running your own business.

3.3 Find Yourself a Mentor

If you have the good fortune of meeting a travel writer whom you respect and admire, try to cultivate a friendship with that person. Chances are, if the two of you are compatible, he or she will gladly share their experience with you as you go along. You can be a tremendous help to that person and they will benefit by seeing how far they've come by talking to you.

CHAPTER 4

Travel Writing Techniques

4.1 General Tips

As you develop your writing style, you'll learn all sorts of techniques for making your text read better. For starters, keep the following in mind:

1. *Write About People, Places, and Things You Like*

There will undoubtedly be times in your life when you'll be asked to write about subjects you really don't like. Of course, you won't necessarily be in a position to turn down work. Few writers are. Still, as often as possible, seek out work that feels close to your heart. If you love the north—pine trees and invigoratingly fresh air, shiny lakes and wool sweaters, cabins and wood-burning stoves—let editors know that. Your fondness for a subject is one of the best qualifications you can have.

2. *Keep a File of Your Observances*

Every time you witness something amusing, saddening, or otherwise thought-provoking, write it down and save it. You never know when you can use it in an article.

3. *Be As Specific As Possible*

As often as possible, use details rather than general descriptions. For example, rather than saying "the scenery was beautiful," describe it: "There were sailboats majestically gliding in the wind, Victorian houses lined up as if contestants in a beauty contest."

4. *The Hamburger Meat Theory*

Sometimes writers—especially new writers—will agonize over a work so much that they destroy it. When writing anything, keep in mind that articles are like hamburger meat. If you handle them too much, they get ruined.

5. *Write As Fast as You Can*

Staring at a blank computer screen can be enormously intimidating. To get started, write what you know about the subject as quickly as you can, not stopping to go back and read or look up a word or a fact. If there are areas or just words you must research before writing, indicate that the information is to come. For example: The Old Town in Stockholm dates back to 0000, the buildings are all 0000 style, and made of stone.

Keep going as long as you can. Don't stop for coffee. Don't stop to throw the clothes in the dryer. Once you've said all you can say, then you can take a break. Afterwards, perhaps even the next day, go back to the file and start filling in the facts and rewriting.

A chunk of copy is a great motivator for writers.

6. *Write in the Active Voice*

Writing in the active voice is quite simply the most direct way to describe anything. Don't allow yourself to use the passive unless absolutely necessary.

7. *Use Only One Exclamation Mark a Year*

Unless the style of the magazine you are on assignment for calls for intermittent exclamation marks, avoid using them as much as possible. Your words alone should be assembled to express the excitement of the situation or description.

8. *Choose the Right Word*

Every single word you use must earn its place on your page. If you can't think of the exact word you want, leave a blank until it comes to mind.

9. *The Suitcase Theory*

When you write an article, think of it as a suitcase. Pack as light as you can. Take only what you need. Write only what needs to be written.

10. *No Experience Is a Wasted Experience*

A novelist friend of mine told me that at one point in his life he was so broke that he took a huge pile of old boxing magazines that he had collected to New York City, spread them out on a sidewalk, and sold them to passersby. As he told the story, his face lit up. He said he met many interesting people that had boxed or watched boxing over the years. In fact, later on, he returned again just for the experience.

As a writer, always keep all your mental doors and windows wide open. If you get an invitation to go to the racetrack but you hate horse races, go. Go if only to look for anecdotes, similes, and metaphors.

11. *Read Aloud*

Once you've written something—a paragraph, a page, an entire article—read it aloud. If it's too wordy, you'll stumble over words. If sentences are too choppy, it'll sound abrupt. If it's well done, you'll feel proud and fueled to carry on.

12. *Save All Research Material*

When writing a travel story, you'll undoubtedly collect many brochures, maps, and notes from interviews. Keep everything in a file for at least six months after the work goes to press.

13. *Set Goals*

Always have short and long-term goals in the works. At the beginning of the week, jot down how much you plan to write. A page a day? A chapter a day? Be realistic.

At the beginning of the year—or at anytime—write down long-term goals. Write down which publications you will try to get published in. Write down how much money you want to make. Write down how often you plan to meet with editors and publishers.

The Big P—Procrastination

Call it writer's block, call it laziness, call it fatigue, call it whatever you like. The fact is that successful writers procrastinate as much as anyone else. One of my friends told me that you can always tell what stage of procrastination he is in by how clean his apartment is. If the bathroom tiles shine, the deadline is probably the next day and he hasn't started the piece yet.

Sometimes we need to procrastinate. While we're doing the things one does when they procrastinate—putting pennies in penny rolls, baking cookies, playing tennis—ideas are often ruminating. It's important to give yourself this gestation time.

Many writers thrive under the pressure that inevitably comes once they've procrastinated for some time. Suddenly, there's great anxiety as to whether they can make their deadline. This can be both motivating and debilitating. As you progress in your profession, learn to identify your own patterns. If you constantly wait until the last minute and then become an inconsolable mess for days as you try to write, it may not be worth it. If you enjoy the peaks and valleys, and your cohabitants don't object, do as you please. Allowing yourself to procrastinate is one of the beauties of being a self-employed writer.

However, here are some tips to avoid problematic procrastination (translation: procrastinating so much you miss deadlines):

1. *Start your day by turning on your computer*

This puts you under some obligation to at least start a file or pull up one you could be working on.

2. *Give yourself easy deadlines*

Decide that all you must do is write half a page before lunch or one entire page for the day.

3. *Use a working lead or don't write a lead at all.*
Sometimes we get too hung up working on a perfect lead. Do the bulk of the piece first and then go back.

4. *Write in your journal or write a letter to a friend*
Sometimes by writing something else, we activate the desire to write.

5. *Don't let a day go by without writing a sentence*

6. *Set up writing hours*
If you write best in the morning, set aside these hours for writing only. No phone calls, no fact-checking a completed article, no bookkeeping.

7. *Read*
Sometimes reading inspires us to write.

8. *Solve the problem*
Often we procrastinate because we dread writing something that may have problems. For example, we may be afraid that we won't get the material we need. This can lead to even greater problems. The best thing you can possibly do is tackle it immediately.

9. *Allow yourself time out*
Go have lunch with your sister. Go play a set of tennis. Go plant the basil. Sometimes we need to just indulge ourselves.

Part Three

TRAVELING IN ORDER TO WRITE ABOUT IT

CHAPTER 5

Starting Out: How to Travel for Your First Story

5.1 Write About Your Hometown

Many people assume that travel writers spend most of their time traveling, especially to exotic faraway places. And of course, most do. However, you don't necessarily have to travel to get started as a travel writer. You could write a travel article about your hometown. If you have lived somewhere for some time, you are probably an expert on inside information. You probably know where to find the best and most affordable restaurants. You probably know when to avoid visiting certain museums because of crowds.

The object is to find an interesting angle and then a publication that would feature it. For example, you might write a piece about the inns in your area and sell it to a travel magazine or combine an inn story with a roundup of restaurants and pitch it to a food magazine. If you happen to live in a popular tourist destination like New York City, you already have eager readers all over the world. Perhaps you could write a piece about the New York delis or eating dim sum in Chinatown. If you happen to be a self-proclaimed expert on the city's gardens or its stained glass windows—all the better.

If you live in a sleepy, uninteresting community, coming up

with an angle can be considerably more challenging. However, there are always angles to be found. For example, let's say your town has a profusion of flea markets and tag sales where a smart shopper can unearth all sorts of rare American-made baubles. This could be very interesting to the foreign traveler, to a collector, or a cross-country traveler looking for points of interest along his/her route. Perhaps your town is known for its bingo games. You could write an article about the characters that play, the passion they have for the game, and the camaraderie that goes along with it.

5.2 Take a Working Vacation

Just about any vacation—whether it's your honeymoon or the annual family trip—can be turned into a travel story. Ideally, you could write a first-person journal of your trip. However, these articles are often the hardest to sell unless you happen to be a celebrity or well-known writer. But they're not impossible. If you are spending a week on Barbados in a rented villa with your kids, your story could appeal to any of the magazines or newspapers that run articles about traveling with children. Your honeymoon in the Poconos would fit right into a bridal publication.

If not first person, you could write a second or third person piece about an aspect of the place you are visiting—its antique shops, its seafood restaurants, or scenic driving tours in the area. Though it sounds easy, this on-location research requires a considerable amount of work. It is necessary to visit and study every place you want to write about.

5.3 Write About a Business Trip

Let's say you're going to be in Cleveland for a conference. Take notes on the restaurants you eat in, the museums you visit, your hotel. Consider staying on a day or two to attend an aviation show or take a walking tour. Play tourist. When you return home, write a feature, a featurette, a blurb, a restaurant review. Send all of them out to publications you think might be interested.

CHAPTER 6

Press Trips

6.1 Press Trips: What Are They?

Most travel editors and successful travel writers are constantly being asked to go on press trips. These are "comped" junkets in which the editor or writer is expected to write about the place they visit.

The trips are often organized by public relations firms that represent hotel properties, tourism boards, airlines, or other travel industry clients. Sometimes they are hosted directly by a country's government, by an airline, or by a hotel. Basically, the host's objective is to familiarize the writer with the destination, the mode of transportation, or an event taking place so that they'll in turn write favorably about it.

Press trips can include anywhere from two travel writers to a couple of dozen, and can last anywhere from a day to a month. They can include both magazine and newspaper editors and writers as well as TV and radio reporters. Some may invite just travel writers. Others may invite a combination of food writers, sports writers, ski writers—what have you.

6.2 The Drawbacks of Press Trips

For someone starting out as a travel writer or someone writing a very generic piece, an all-expense paid trip can be a wonderful way to visit a new city, a new state, a new island, or a new country. But the trips are rarely organized so that the writer can truly see a place as one of their readers would.

For one thing, press get V.I.P. treatment on press trips. They are usually given the best rooms, the best views, a bottle of champagne, and a basket of fruit. They are often driven around by one of the destination's best tour guides, introduced to chefs, innkeepers, and government officials. On some trips, the writers are so cut off from the realities of the area that they never change money to the local currency and never bother looking at a local map.

Another problem with press trips is that not all writers enjoy being rubberbanded into a bunch like stalks of asparagus. Customarily, each individual has his/her own assignment to research. With a press group, an adventure writer may find him/herself traipsing through conference room after conference room so the writer from *Conferences and Conventions Magazine* can get his story, or being forced to look at the honeymoon suite in every hotel for the writer from *Country Bride.*

On top of this, there is almost always a "bed bug" in the group: The one person that chronically complains, that chronically holds up the group, that chronically annoys everyone. At meal times, it's usually a scramble to find the seat furthest away from this character.

The Do's and Don'ts of Press Trip Travel

DO

- Do request to see the itinerary before accepting a trip. If there are going to be a lot of stops you have no use for, it may be best not to go.
- Do plan to spend a lot of time socializing. You'll most likely spend every meal with the other writers as well as hotel managers, tourism officials, and public relations representatives.
- Do check beforehand whether the publication you're planning to write for accepts articles written from free or subsidized trips.

DON'T

- Don't expect to have a lot of free time. On many press trips, writers are rushed from event to event, from attraction to attraction.
- Don't count on having lots of time for interviews and in-depth research.
- Don't expect to walk away with a comprehensive knowledge of the destination.
- Don't assume you can order whatever you like from a menu. Often, a "special meal" is prepared for a press group.

6.3 How to Get Invited on Press Trips

Once you get established as a travel writer, you will undoubtedly get more trip invitations than you can possibly take. This comes in due time, through making contacts throughout the industry.

To get the very first invitations, it's necessary to cultivate contacts in the area or areas you are interested in covering. For example, if you have great interest in writing about the Caribbean, start by finding out which public relations firms represent the various islands and hotels. This can be ascertained by calling the individual tourist boards and asking for the name of their public relations firm. You will soon find that for almost all of the islands in the Caribbean, there is a public relations representative. There are also public relations representatives for all the major hotels and sometimes some of the smaller ones. Most of the big ones have 800 numbers which you can call and ask for the public relations firm, most of which are located in major U.S. cities.

If you've written anything about the Caribbean (from a trip you took on your own funds), send it off to the various public relations firms introducing yourself. Here's an example of what you may write:

Executive's Name
Exact Title
Public Relations Firm
Street Address
City, State, Zip

Dear (Executive's Name):

I thought you might like to see this article I wrote for *Caribbean Vacations Magazine* on the resorts of Jamaica.

I understand you represent the British Virgin Islands and thought you might be interested in working with me. At the moment, I am developing a couple of British Virgin Island story ideas and plan to pitch them to several national publications. If you have the time, I'd like to meet and discuss this further.

I'll give you a call in a week.

Sincerely,

Your Name

This shows that you have interest in their destination and will most likely add you to a list to be considered for press trips.

6.4 The Politics of Press Trips

Mention that you are taking a press trip these days, and in some circles you'll hear all sorts of snickers. At present, this is a highly controversial subject in the travel writing industry. Many major newspapers and some of the top travel magazines have no-press-trips policies. For some, you must sign a form saying you did not take a subsidized trip. The reasoning is simple: how can a writer get a true story if he/she is a non-paying guest?

Still, the controversy lies in the fact that some of these magazine mastheads are made up of editors who have spent years flying around the world for free. And in fact, at one magazine publishing company, the editors and writers are forbidden to take subsidized travel, yet editors and writers from other magazines in the same company travel for free routinely.

The problem with the no-freebie policy is that few travel writers can afford to travel to all the places they are required to write about. Unless you have another income, the money you spend on travel each year could exceed the money you earn from travel writing.

So what does the travel writer do? Fortunately, there are enough publications that allow writers to take press trips, and in fact, have come to depend on it. Some publications provide expense accounts for their assignments. Another approach is to pay for your own trip, and write many different stories about it for a variety of publications.

CHAPTER 7

Traveling Solo for Free

7.1 What It Takes

Many travel writers prefer to travel alone or with a photographer, friend, or spouse rather than join a press group. That way, they move along at their own pace, stopping only where they must or want to stop, and taking necessary time for interviews and other on-site research.

A veteran travel writer can basically go anywhere and practically spend less money than they would if they stayed home. These writers have established contacts throughout the industry and are widely published.

Early on in your travel writing career, this is not as easy, but is possible, provided you have a confirmed assignment and are planning to mention your various hosts in your article.

Through careful planning and research, you can usually arrange for complimentary transportation to and from the destination, a guided tour around the destination, accommodations, and some admission fees and activities. Most meals would have to be paid for out of your own pocket.

7.2 Arranging Free Travel: Step-by-Step

Let's say a magazine publisher has asked you to write an article about Barbados. Here's one way to go about getting the trip paid for.

Step One: Introductions

Have your editor or publisher send you a letter of introduction in addition to a contract. When you receive it, make several copies. The letter should say something along these lines on the publication's letterhead:

To Whom It May Concern:

This will introduce Cathleen King, who has been assigned to write an article about "Barbados in the Off-Season" which will appear in our April, 1993 issue. Ms. King will be traveling to Barbados to gather accurate information. Any assistance you can give her would be greatly appreciated by us.

Thank you.

Sincerely,

(The Editor's or Publisher's Name and Title)

Sometimes an editor will send an elaborate assignment letter in lieu of a contract which will spell out the details of the assignment.

If you're going to circulate this letter, cross out information regarding the fee they agree to pay.

Step Two: Do some preliminary research

Look through guidebooks and travel articles about Barbados. Figure out which sights you'll want to see, which inns or hotels are most appropriate for the readership of the publication you're on assignment for. Have a rough idea of how many days you would need to stay.

Step Three: Contact the public relations office

This can be done by calling the Barbados Board of Tourism first and asking for their public relations firm. Introduce yourself to the public relations representative and tell them that you are planning to visit the island. Follow up by faxing or mailing them the letter of introduction or assignment letter along with any published articles you may have written.

Step Four: Plan your itinerary

It's extremely important at this point to have a very clear idea as to what you must research while at the destination. Ideally, you should put together a proposed itinerary which includes the hotels, restaurants, and attractions you must see in order to get your story. Otherwise, you leave the guesswork up to the public relations firm and may find yourself staying in inappropriate hotels and eating and spending your time doing inappropriate things. Ideally, you should rough out an itinerary such as the following:

BARBADOS ITINERARY

January 5

Fly from New York to Barbados.

Check into Coral Reef Hotel.

Spend afternoon exploring Bridgetown.

Dinner at Josef's Restaurant.

January 6

Breakfast at hotel

Pick up rental car. Spend day touring northern end of island, stopping at sights and hotels along the way.

Stop for lunch at Atlantis Restaurant.

Return to hotel. Dinner at La Cage aux Folles.

January 7

Spend day touring southern end of island.

Lunch at the Barbados Museum.

Dinner at Witch Doctor Restaurant.

After dinner, check out nightlife at After Dark disco.

January 8

Spend morning touring interior of island.

Lunch at Waterfront Cafe in Bridgetown.

Afternoon at Pelican Village shopping center.

Dinner at Reid's Restaurant.

After dinner, stop by Baxter's Road.

January 9

Early flight back to New York.

Step Five: Touch base with the pr firm

If the public relations firm agreed to help organize your trip, go ahead and send them a copy of the proposed itinerary. Some firms may put you in touch directly with the various airlines and hotels.

Step Six: Contact airline officials

If the public relations firm cannot make the air arrangements—which is not uncommon—it's necessary to contact the airline public relations manager directly. Your best bet is to choose one airline. If they're unable to accommodate you, try others. Usually, you can introduce yourself on the phone and then follow up by sending a copy of the assignment letter, a biography, and travel dates and flights you would like. For example:

Airline Public Relations Executive
Exact Title
Airline
Street Address
City, State, Zip

Dear (Airline Public Relations Executive):

As I briefly explained to you on the telephone, I am writing an article for *Island Discoveries* magazine on Barbados. It is published quarterly and has a national circulation of more than 350,000.

I will be traveling to the island January 5–9 and wondered if it would be possible to obtain a comp round-trip ticket. The article will include information on getting to the island and mention Air Barbados as a major carrier. I have tentatively made reservations on the following flights.

January 5th: Air Barbados 659
JFK 9 A.M.
Barbados 3:01 P.M.

January 9th: Air Barbados 1050
Barbados 3:56 P.M.
JFK 11:48 P.M.

I've enclosed an author's biography for your information. Please let me know if you need any additional information.

Sincerely,

Your Name

Step Seven: Contact hotels and other accommodations
If the public relations firm advises you to contact the hotels and inns on your own, introduce yourself and the assignment as you did to the airline official. Again, you are best off requesting a room with one hotel rather than several for the same nights. If they cannot provide a comp room, try others.

Step Eight: Wait patiently
This process can take anywhere from a couple of days to a couple of weeks.

CHAPTER
8

Travel Expense Accounts

8.1 Who Gives Them, Who Gets Them

Whether you will be offered a travel budget or not will depend completely on which publication you are writing for. By in large, most publications do not "send" new writers on trips and, in fact, many publications never "send" any writers on trips. They expect the writers to use their own resources. Some include the expense of travel in the overall fee. Always ask, however. Ask if they can at least contribute by paying for the airfare or another expense.

CHAPTER 9

On-Location Research

9.1 Getting Your Story

If you imagine yourself traveling to all sorts of exotic locales and spending hours lounging around beaches and bars—you're in for a bit of a jolt. Of course, as a travel writer, you will most likely visit flabbergastingly beautiful places, and you will inevitably find yourself on yachts, on camels, in gliders, in hot-air balloons—you name it. Still, a travel writer does the bulk of his/her research when on location.

This is work after all, and not a vacation—even if it is Tahiti. Depending on your assignment, you may have to cram a pile of interviews into a day or two. You may have to drive around the island to see every attraction, hotel, and restaurant. When you do go to the beach, it's usually with notebook in hand to record the color of the sand, the types of beachgoers, the view all around. When you stop at a bar, you can't forget to note down that it has a thatched roof, that the floor is sand, and that the resident cat Charlie greets everyone at the door with a wave of the paw. Admittedly, this can be fun. However, your mind is always at work when on the road, unless you have a very specialized assignment and can get your information otherwise.

9.2 Tools of the Travel Writer's Trade

Every writer has his/her own preference on how they like to record notes while on the road. Here are some examples.

A Notebook: Whether you feel comfortable with a tiny notebook or a legal pad, some assemblage of paper is usually necessary. When you return home, you can either save the entire notebook or tear out the pages and file them, or transfer them to computer files.

A Tape Recorder: Needless to say, the lighter and smaller, the better. Consider investing in a microcassette recorder which you can attach to your belt. Tape recorders are especially good if you're interviewing or if you're driving a lot. As you cruise along, you can rattle on about what the scenery is like. Some writers even start their stories on tape recorders while driving. With a tape recorder you can also record sounds such as local music, local accents, bird songs, animal sounds, and any other audios you may come across. When it comes to writing your story, these can help evoke the feeling of being back at the place.

If you're taking tours, you can record the tour guide's complete commentary. Some writers record all of their notes on a tape recorder and later transcribe them into a computer file. Other writers complain that the transcribing is too time-consuming.

A Camera: A lot of times you'll see travel writers clicking away with a little point-and-shoot camera as if they're on a family outing. This is just another form of note-taking. When it comes time to write the story, photographs can clearly bring it all back. Of course, it's a little more expensive than writing or taping notes.

A Laptop Computer: More and more writers write their stories on the road. Some even take them along just to key in all their notes at the end of each day. The notebook-sized laptops can run for as long as three hours between battery charges and are surprisingly inexpensive (at press time, under $2000).

A Currency Convertor or Calculator: Especially when traveling abroad, you'll find yourself doing a lot of arithmetic, whether converting francs into pounds or kilometers into miles.

Address/Phone Book: It's important to be able to contact people back home as well as in the destinations you are visiting. Before leaving home, be sure you have all the numbers you may need. If you have an electronic calculator/address book, all the better.

A Sturdy and Spacious Satchel: As you travel around various destinations, you will inevitably collect brochures, maps, and booklets as well as any books you might buy *en route.*

9.3 What to Pack

Not every travel writer packs as efficiently as the travel writer in *The Accidental Tourist*, who never traveled with more than a slim carry-on. In fact, many travel writers suffer from incurable over-packing-itis.

One way to avoid over-packing is to limit yourself to the use of carry-on luggage. Many travel writers do this anyway to avoid having to wait for baggage at airports. However, if you're traveling for a week or more, chances are a carry-on just won't do it.

When packing, I always start with a copy of my itinerary. I go through it and see how many formal events I'll need to dress up for, whether I'll be doing any hiking or horseback riding, or anything else that requires special clothing. I make sure I'm covered for these outings and then pack as many casual pieces I can squeeze into my bag. Casual meaning the clothes I can do my research in.

If I'm in the Caribbean, that means light skirts and tops or shorts. If I'm in Scandinavia during Christmastime, that means wool skirts and pants, sweaters and warm socks.

I try to pack as monochromatically as possible, so everything can be mixed and matched. For variation, I throw in scarves, belts, and other accessories.

I'm always well-covered in the footwear department: comfortable flats for walking, boots for hiking, dress shoes for evenings, sneakers for playing tennis or working out in the resort's gym, flip-flops for the hotel room, the beach, and pool areas.

I also always take a light cotton robe for mornings when I order room service.

9.4 Things You Might Not Have Thought to Pack

Extra luggage: Just in case you go on a shopping spree, have a light nylon bag you can uncrumple and fill.

Heavy-duty tape: A roll of wide heavy-duty tape comes in very handy to reinforce boxes and bags.

A tiny stapler: For keeping loose receipts and small sheets of paper together efficiently.

Band-Aids: It's always a good idea to have a supply on hand.

Reading material: For long flights, airport and train station waits, and other stretches of time, take along a couple of novels and other books that have nothing to do with your research.

A flashlight: Whether you use it during a power failure or to find your way back to your hotel on an unlit road, a flashlight will come in handy.

A Swiss Army knife: For slicing bread, for opening wine, for cutting thread—it's a traveler's must.

Part Four

SELLING YOUR WORK

CHAPTER 10

Preparing a Story Idea

10.1 Coming Up With the Initial Idea

Few writers sit down at an empty computer screen and wait for ideas to come to mind. Most have files—or piles—of ideas that they've thought about from time to time. Sometimes a friend, a public relations executive, or another writer will pass along a good idea. Sometimes a writer will go some place to research one story and find half a dozen other angles to cover. Ideas come when you're waiting in line at the subway token booth, when you're in the shower, when you're writing about something else. They come while brainstorming with friends and other writers.

Start a file—or a pile—that's for ideas. These do not have to be kept in any particular fashion. They can be press releases, photographs, other articles. That way, when it comes down to pitching story ideas, you already have some to work with. Choose subjects you personally feel comfortable with. As O. Henry said, "Write what makes you happy."

10.2 Determining Whether the Idea Is Marketable

Once you have an article idea, ask yourself the following questions: Is it really interesting? Is it overdone? Is it going to be dated too soon? Can people afford this kind of trip these days? Is this a destination that could be politically shaky? Are people still associating this place with some major earthquake, or other natural disaster?

10.3 Identify Your Readership

After you've established that the idea is good, try to picture your readers. Would they be upscale travelers with a money's-no-object attitude? European students looking for budget finds? Honeymooners? Would they be senior citizens or teenagers? Young parents? Who would be interested in reading about this?

10.4 Choose Publications to Pitch To

Once you determine who your readers are, stop in a good newsstand or your local library and glance over the magazine racks. Which magazine reaches the audience that would be interested in this particular subject? Start with the major categories. Would it belong in a women's magazine? A home furnishing magazine? A sporting magazine? What about newspapers? Could you get it in a major Sunday travel section? In your hometown weekly?

Let's say it could be in a women's magazine. Take a look at all the women's magazines you can. If it's a straight travel piece, make sure the magazine has a travel section or column. If it combines food and travel or another area, check to see that there is an appropriate place for it somewhere in the magazine.

Look at the other features and featurettes in the magazine. Would these readers be interested in your piece? Could these readers afford what you're suggesting? Is your idea too rough and rugged for them? It has to be a perfect fit.

10.5 Study the Publications

If there are three or four publications you feel it could possible run in, take time to study their styles. Is it light and bright? Is it dense? Is it academic or playful? Are articles long or very brief? Are they first, second, or third person? It is important to understand the style at this point so that you can write your proposal in the same tone. Later on, you will have to study the style even more in order to write a complete article.

CHAPTER 11

Getting the Assignment

11.1 Query Letters and Proposals

When you first start out as a travel writer, you'll have to join the masses of anonymous query letter senders. This can be very disconcerting at times. Nevertheless, the key is to persevere. Expect rejection, it's inevitable. It can come in the form of never hearing from the editor again or getting an impersonal "thanks but no thanks" note signed by the department assistant. Every now and then you might be surprised by a somewhat encouraging rejection letter written by the editor him/herself.

Avoid using all sorts of clever tactics to get an editor's attention. When sending a proposal, the best way to get their attention is to enclose anything that you have had published—even if it's a short article in the local Audubon chapter newsletter—along with a query letter, your biography, and a self-addressed stamped envelope (if you want your materials back). Many editors are very insecure and feel that if somebody had enough faith in you to publish a piece you did, you're probably okay.

Of course, if you're just starting out, you don't have clips. Don't despair. A well written query letter can be a very good indication of how well you write.

When writing a query letter, keep these guidelines in mind:

1. *Customize the query to the publication you are addressing*

Many writers come up with ideas and simultaneously send them to dozens of publications, never taking time out to check if the subject is really appropriate for the various readerships. Nothing annoys editors more. You may even get a nasty note in response.

2. *Be brief and to the point*

3. *Write simply, but impeccably*

Your writing style can come out even in a few short sentences. It gives the editor an idea of how you think.

4. *Suggest several stories*

Editors like to see lots of ideas, not just one.

5. *Present yourself professionally*

Have letterhead made up with the title of your choice (Travel Writer, Editor/Writer, Journalist/Author, Writer/Photographer, Reporter).

The following information should be included:

1. A synopsis of the idea and why it would appeal to this particular publication's readership.
2. A suggested format and length of the article—a 1000-word first-person travel diary, a 3000-word destination feature, a 200-word vignette for a column the publication already has.
3. Any credentials you may have that are specifically related to the subject you are proposing.

If you have suggestions for photography or illustrations, that can be included as well.

Here are some sample query letters. Allow about two weeks before making follow up calls.

Example #1

Travel Editor's Name
Exact Title
Publication
Street Address
City, State, and Zip

Dear (Travel Editor's Name):

Congratulations on being named the travel editor of *Wanderings* magazine. Your first two issues were absolutely beautiful.

I thought you might like to know that I will be spending three months in the state of Maine researching a guidebook. While there, I would be happy to research a story for *Wanderings.* Do any of the following appeal?

1. Active Maine
This would be a 3000-word roundup of participatory ways in which visitors can enjoy the coast and woods of Maine. I would include a brief description of windjammer cruises, bicycle tours, sailing schools, canoe trips, whale-watching excursions, great walks, deep-sea fishing trips, golf courses and hot-air balloon rides. I would also include information on the L. L. Bean workshops, which cover everything from cross-country ski lessons and golf instruction to lectures on survival in the Maine woods, making soap, tanning hides, building fly rods, cooking small game, and fishing for Atlantic salmon.

2. The Other Maine
I think a third-person piece focusing on the real Maine, not the tourist side, would be of great appeal to your readers. It would be rich in detail and include quotes by residents, some of whom are descendants of Scandinavian immigrants and others who are former Wall Street executives.

In addition, I could provide service information such as suggested driving tours, staying places (including full-of-character New England inns and multi-faceted seaside resorts), restaurants (especially great lobster spots), and attractions. It would run about 3000 words.

3. Bush Country, U.S.A.
I will be spending some time at Hope Island which is a spectacularly handsome house on its own island not far from the summer White House. It's available for groups of ten or more and offers an array of activities including fishing, duck hunting, and sailing. Guests can also take boat picnics to L. L. Bean in Freeport. I understand the food is nonpareil, the rooms simple and lovely, and the hospitality unending. I could cover this hotel on its own or incorporate it into a broader article on New England accommodations.

I will be leaving for Maine on June 3rd. Let me know if you're interested in one of the aforementioned ideas, and I can schedule my research accordingly. I'm open to discuss other angles as well.

Sincerely,

Your Name

Example #2

Travel Editor's Name
Exact Title
Publication
Street Address
City, State, and Zip

Dear (Travel Editor's Name):

Having read and studied your magazine over the last several years, I understand that you frequently run articles about various destinations around Florida. A native Floridian, I have travelled extensively in the state and have written about it for various newspapers (see enclosed clips). Could I interest you in one of the following articles?

1. Key to the Keys
Too many visitors skim over the northernmost Florida Keys on their way to Key West. But the real key here is to take your time. These islands (45 are linked by the Overseas Highway) are little destinations in themselves. This would be a 2000-word feature focusing on the various highlights of each.

2. Miami Nice
Now that the TV cameras are long gone and the last of *Miami Vice's* props have been auctioned off, what's the story with Miami? Lots of good things. Though the prime-time show made the city out to be a battlefield of drug dealers, it also generated a revitalization, especially in the formerly run-down Art Deco District where much of the series was filmed. The square-mile area in SoBe (short for South Beach) is not only filled with Easter egg-colored deco buildings, but is now a magnet for the young, hip, and artsy with its outdoor cafes

and fast-forward night clubs. Jet-set South Americans and Europeans are swooping in by the planeload and a whole new generation of New Yorkers have staked out beach apartments here.

This would be a 3000-word feature about the new Miami.

I will give you a call in a couple of weeks to discuss this further. Thank you for your time.

Sincerely,

Your Name

Example #3

Travel Editor's Name
Exact Title
Publication
Street Address
City, State, and Zip

Dear (Travel Editor's name):

I have just returned from a year-long stay in Iceland and thought the following ideas would be very appropriate for your readership. Please let me know if you'd like me to elaborate on any of them:

1. Consuming Interests: Icelandic Cuisine
Fifteen years ago, there were only three "decent" restaurants

in Reykjavik, now there are about fifty. As a result, Icelandic restaurants are becoming more and more competitive and the cuisine has become quite sophisticated.

This would be a 1000-word food piece focusing on the various Icelandic dishes for your "Foods Around the World" column.

2. Touring Iceland: Civilized Adventure Travel
One does not have to be a backpacker, an experienced rock climber, or even an adventurous type to tour Iceland. This phenomenal country—which is still being born—can be seen very easily by driving around its ring road in about a week's time.

This would be a first-person story about my own experiences of traveling around Iceland. I would include information on hotels and inns as well as restaurants along the way. I picture this as a 2000-word feature.

3. Looking Up to Iceland
How did this little nation become one of the most progressive countries in the world? Since 1980, Iceland has had the world's first directly-elected woman president, about 30 percent of its children are born out of wedlock with absolutely no stigma attached by society, and women have never changed their names in marriage.

On top of that, life expectancy in Iceland is eighty years for women and seventy-four for men—one of the highest in the world. According to the Icelanders, this can largely be attributed to the diet, which consists predominately of fish, the lack of pollution (since there is little agriculture, there are no herbicides and pesticides), and the fact that the country's heat and energy is largely produced geothermally and hydroelectrically.

I would like to discuss this country's amazing accomplishments in your "Travel Potpourri" column. It would be about 1000 words long.

I'll give you a call in a couple of weeks to discuss this further.

Sincerely,

Your Name

Every now and then, an editor will ask to see a more elaborate description or outline of a story idea. This step is actually the most crucial step of the whole process. You have their interest and a better chance of selling your story. It's also a very time consuming step because you have to hammer out the direction of the piece. Nevertheless, the better you organize it at this point, the better off you are when it comes down to writing the actual copy. Here are some sample proposals:

Example #1

Travel Editor's Name
Exact Title
Publication
Street Address
City, State, and Zip

Dear (Travel Editor's Name):

Your premier issue looks great. Congratulations. As promised, here's a more detailed proposal for my Maine piece. Please let me know what you think.

1. The lead: I thought I'd start off with an anecdote about President Bush's summer vacation in his house in Kennebunkport. The little resort town—which some now call Kenne*bush*port—was crawling with reporters trying to get a story angle on his vacation. However, with helicopters whirling overhead and a flotilla of Secret Service agents standing guard, not much could possibly go wrong and make news. So, the summer's newspaper stories revolved around the President's fishing misfortunes. Practically every day for the duration of his vacation, he would go out fishing and come back empty-handed. It became the talk of New England. In fact, The Portland Press Herald had a "Fishwatch" (complete with a "No Bluefish" logo, a bluefish with a big X through it), in which they kept a running tally totting the President's daily catch.

2. From there, I would talk about how many New England families have huge summer houses (not quite as opulent, but certainly as expensive—and expansive—as the Newport mansions) on islands and along the coast of Maine. Most

summer homeowners choose Maine because of its natural beauty. There are hundreds of spruce and fir-covered islands, all sorts of exotic birds, and magnificently beautiful sailing and boating waters. Maine is known as the Vacation State and indeed, offers many opportunities to vacate cluttered lives.

3. Unfortunately, much of the Maine waterfront is privately owned, and therefore largely inaccessible to the average tourist. However, visitors can have access by staying in certain inns and hotels. One outstanding example is Hope Island, an 18-bedroom house propped up on its own 85 acre island in Casco Bay (not far from the Bush compound). This formerly private home is now available for groups of up to twenty-five people. I found it especially appealing because it simulated the experience of having a summer home in Maine (of course, without the headaches). There is a staff that's very attentive, though not fawning. The chef—an import from a Caribbean resort—does wonderful things with the fresh fish and lobster that are delivered by local lobstermen and fishermen daily. He also prepares fish caught by visitors.

Guests can occupy themselves doing all the Mainese things, such as sailing, boating, and bird-watching or just taking in the scenery from the verandah. They can also be whizzed over to the mainland on one of the island's launches to shop in L. L. Bean and the multitude of factory outlets that make up the town of Freeport. On top of that, there's golf and tennis, and Portland, Maine's most vibrant city, nearby.

4. Finally, I could mention a handful of other outstanding inns or hotels on the coast of Maine.

For a sidebar, I suggest one of the following. Let me know which one most appeals to you.

L. L. Bean: This American institution is still going strong. It was started by an avid outdoorsman who built up a mail-order business with his Maine hunting shoe. Today, the quality of the rugged outdoor clothes and equipment is legendary, and the store—a huge mall-like building—is open 24 hours a day. L. L. Bean's success is largely due to the fact that they market the image of Maine (outdoors, fresh-air, healthy) and the Maine people (hard-working, rugged, independent). In this sidebar, I would tell the L. L. Bean story and report current statistics on earnings and such.

Galleries of Maine: The countryside of Maine is dotted with studios and galleries of well-known or up-and-coming artists and craftspeople. For example, on Deer Isle alone, visitors find the studios of Ronald Hayes Pearson (sterling silver and gold jewelry), Kathy Woell (handwoven garments in wool and mohair yarns), and William Mor (contemporary stoneware and folk pottery). In this sidebar, I would give a listing of some of the best with brief descriptions, addresses, and phone numbers.

I look forward to hearing from you.

Sincerely,

Your Name

Example #2

Travel Editor's Name
Exact Title
Publication
Street Address
City, State, and Zip

Dear (Travel Editor's Name):

Here is a complete outline for the Europe section I have proposed. Please let me know at your earliest convenience if you'd like to go ahead with the project.

GETTING YOUR MONEY'S WORTH IN EUROPE

Overview: This section will be chock-full of tips and hints on how visitors can stretch their dollars while traveling to and around Europe. It will emphasize the fact that one need not economize on comfort while cutting costs, especially if they do a little homework in advance and—in some cases—pre-pay their trips.

Proposed Outline

1. The lead will be written to capture the readers' interest in saving money while traveling to Europe in style.
2. The piece will be broken up into the following categories.

   A. Taking Off
   This section will be filled with tips on how one can go about finding the best airfares to Europe. Some specific airlines and prices (as well as air/land packages) will be mentioned. It will explain the advantages of purchasing

tickets in advance, but will also mention some special last minute deals that are available.

B. Arriving (possibly a chart format)
Sometimes a train from the airport to the center of a European city is not only cheaper than a taxi, but much faster and incredibly convenient to use. This will list the various airports that have exceptionally good train service to their city centers.

C. Getting Around Town (chart)
Many European cities have special discount cards that are good for unlimited travel on public transportation (the Paris Metro Pass, the London Visitor Travelcard, the Helsinki Card, etc). This chart will include information on how much they cost, how much of a discount they offer, how many days they are effective for, and where they can be purchased.

D. From Country to Country
This section will cover the various cost-cutting ways to travel within Europe.

Rail Deals: (chart) This will be a small chart listing the different rail passes available including the Eurailpass, the Eurail Flexipass, and the fairly new European East Pass which provides unlimited first class train travel through Austria, Czechoslovakia, Hungary, and Poland.

Wheel Deals: This will include tips on renting a car. Is it cheaper to make arrangements before leaving the States? Should you use a big U.S. firm like Hertz or Avis or a local car rental place?

To Fly or Not to Fly? Though intra-Europe airfares are

higher than in the U.S., there are some excursion fares available. If examples are available, they will be mentioned.

E. Checking In

This section will include innumerable tips on how to save on overnight accommodations such as the following:

During July and August, several major city hotels—such as the Inter-Continental and Hilton International—offer substantially lower summer rates at their properties. These rates can be 20, 30, even 50 percent off standard rates. Sample prices will be included.

After mid-September, in the resort hotels along the Mediterranean, prices are slashed as much as 50 percent. Examples, if available, will be provided.

In some European cities, you can rent an apartment and save considerably. For example, in Prague, a one-bedroom suite complete with housekeeping and concierge service runs between $105 and $155 a night; a two-bedroom, $135–$210 (price differs according to season).

In addition, many European hotels are offering special incentives to attract guests. For example, one hotel in London has gone so far as to offer the sterling rate at the dollar equivalent. Several others are offering two nights for the price of one.

F. Consuming Interests

This section will focus on ways to save while dining out in Europe. For example:

Highly regarded restaurants all over Europe offer *prix fixe* luncheon menus at a fraction of the cost of an *à la carte* dinner and though the selection may not be as extensive, the food is the same.

Some museum restaurants have surprisingly good lunches and are remarkably reasonable, such as The British Museum.

Avoid places that offer "tourist menus." They're often pricey and the food can be lamentable.

At most restaurant/bars, it's cheaper to stand at the bar for a cup of coffee or a mug of beer than to sit at a table.

G. Sightseeing Discounts
This section will mention special discounted passes for European attractions such as the Great British Heritage Pass, which entitles visitors to free admission to about 600 historical attractions (including castles, abbeys, and gardens). The pass costs $45 for 15 days and can be obtained from a travel agent or from the British Travel Bookshop.

H. Free-for-Alls
Not everything has an admission price in Europe. This section will be a roundup of things to do for free including outdoor concerts, summer festivals, churches, changing of the guard ceremonies, design centers, and top museums (such as The British Museum and The National Gallery).

I. In the Market (box)
This will be a small box explaining what VAT shopping refunds are.

J. Currency Concerns
Where's the best place to cash travelers checks? The bank, the railway station, the hotel, the gas stations? How do you get rid of extra coins before crossing a border in Europe? These and other money matters will be addressed in this section.

3. Free Maps, Brochures, and More Information
This will be a list of all the individual European tourist boards along with phone numbers and addresses.

4. Work sheet (if space available)
This work sheet will be designed so the reader can roughly calculate the cost of their European vacation.

I look forward to talking with you.

Sincerely,

Your Name

11.2 On Spec Manuscripts

Sometimes editors will make assignments "on spec" (speculation) which basically means there is no guarantee that they will buy it. This can be risky as you invest a great deal of time researching and writing the actual piece. However, an "on spec" assignment is better than no assignment. It's an opportunity to show them how good a writer you are. Take no shortcuts in producing your finest work when writing on spec.

11.3 Unsolicited Manuscripts

Though you can write articles and feel free to send them to various publications, I suggest you not send them to magazines. Full-length articles showing up on editors' desks often get treated like press releases—tossed or put in some pile never to be seen again for years.

Newspapers, on the other hand, frequently publish unsolicited freelance manuscripts. Your best bet is to send out multiple copies of one article (the customary length for newspapers is about 1000 words) to papers all over the country that have noncompeting markets. Enclose a cover letter and specify that the article is "on a first-rights basis in your circulation area." It's not necessary to follow up with telephone calls. Just sit back and hope checks will come in along with copies of your printed article.

11.4 Telephone Pitches

Once you get established in the business and work regularly with several different editors, you won't have to bother doing so much preliminary selling. In fact, widely-published travel writers routinely call and pitch ideas to three or four editors every time they plan a trip. These editors know their work and generally are happy to know which destinations they're available to cover.

Starting out, however, your best bet is only call in order to follow up on magazine proposals. At that point, if the editor shows some interest, but does not commit, you might wait a few weeks and call again. If they are downright rude—which certainly can happen—move on.

CHAPTER 12

Confirming the Assignment

12.1 Assignment Letters

Once a magazine editor agrees to assign an article to a writer, they'll often send an assignment letter shortly afterwards confirming the terms of the assignment. These, of course, vary from publication to publication but generally include the working title of the article, the issue it is scheduled to appear in, the number of words, the deadline, the rights, the fee, and information about a kill fee if for any reason the article does not run. If one is not automatically sent to you, ask for one to avoid problems down the road. Newspapers generally do not send assignment letters.

12.2 Contracts

Some magazines and all book editors will send contracts in which all the terms of the agreement are clearly stated. The writer is expected to review the contract, sign multiple copies, and return them all to the publisher who in turn will sign and return a copy to the writer. In the case of book contracts, an advance (usually half) is customarily paid upon signing the contract. For most magazines, however, the total amount due is paid when the work is submitted and approved or when it goes to press.

When you receive a contract:

1. Take time to read it over very carefully. If you have an agent, have him or her read it over.
2. If any of the items are problematic, call the editor—or have your agent call—and discuss your concerns. If you both agree an item can be amended, you can usually cross it out and write in the change, and have both parties initial it.

12.3 Copyrights

Since 1976, every article you write is automatically copyrighted, just like a piece of artwork. In your contract, if no rights are mentioned, consider writing in "First North American Serial Rights" which means that you will grant the first publisher the right to publish your story once in North America, but that the publisher does not own the copyright.

12.4 Work for Hire

You'll see these three words frequently in travel guidebook contracts. Basically, they mean that the writer is hired to write a work for the publisher and that the publisher ultimately owns it and can do as they please with it.

12.5 Kill Fees

A kill fee is a percentage of the originally agreed upon fee—usually no more than 30 percent—that a publisher agrees to pay a writer in the event the assigned article doesn't run. The kill fee is paid to the writer who has successfully completed the work. It is important to establish the kill fee in the written contract.

12.6 Legal Advice

Throughout your writing career, you will inevitably have legal questions. If you're a member of a writers' organization (see Appendix B), check to see if they provide free legal advice for members. If you have an agent, contact him or her. In addition, an excellent book to have on hand is *The Writers Legal Companion* (Addison-Wesley Publishing Company, Inc., 1988) by Brad Bunnin and Peter Beren.

CHAPTER 13

Being Asked Back

13.1 Keep Abreast of What's New

In order to develop good story proposals, it's important that the writer keep up with the trends of the industry. Where are people traveling to? Is the Pacific Northwest hot? Is there a trend towards fitness vacations? Are farm vacations taking off? Is Cuba making a comeback? But there are other reasons to keep abreast of what's needed. As a professional travel writer, you will undoubtedly be asked over and over again about your opinion. Though you cannot be required to know everything about every place in the world, you should at least know the major news items.

There are several ways to do this.

1. *Read, read, read*

If you don't have time for entire features, at least scan the pages of the big travel magazines such as *Travel & Leisure, Conde Nast Traveler, National Geographic Traveler*, and *Travel Holiday* each month. If you're interested in women's travel, look at the travel sections of *Vogue, Glamour*, and *Mirabella* (or any of the other women's magazines). If you enjoy writing about travel and food, look at *Gourmet, Food Arts*, and other food magazines. Newspaper travel sections should also be read or scanned.

2. *Go to the movies*

Movies often influence travel trends. Right after *Dances With Wolves* came out, there was an increase in travel to the southwest and—yes, cattle drives for vacations. Find out what movies are coming out, where they were set, who starred in them.

3. *Ask editors and writers*

Make this your opening line during a press reception conversation: "So, where are your readers traveling to these days?"

4. *Look ahead*

Where are the Winter Olympics going to be in 1994? Is there any big anniversary coming up—anywhere? Is there a once-in-a-century eclipse taking place somewhere?

5. *Watch the news*

Is one country inching towards war? Is another country becoming more affordable because of currency devaluation?

6. *Keep an eye on general trends*

Earth awareness. Budget-consciousness. Quality-of-life programs. These are all trends that influence how and where people travel.

13.2 Submitting Articles

Though content is the most important part of any body of material you submit, the mechanics of how you submit it are very important. Pay attention to all of the following for everything you are asked to write.

1. *Confirm manuscript mechanics beforehand*

Would the editor like hard copies? Diskette copies? Are your computers and programs compatible? Would they like text sent by fax? By modem? Always double space, always leave margins of at least one inch on all sides, always print out articles on plain white paper, and always number the pages. Type in upper and lowercase, never all capital letters.

2. *Stick to the assigned length*

If an editor asks for a 1000-word piece, write as close to that as possible. Unless they specifically say that there is great flexibility, do not hand in a piece twice the length or half the length. By the time the assignment is made, the editor has roughly figured out how much space is allotted for it. If you hand in an article or book manuscript that's long, you put yourself in a very vulnerable position since the editor will be forced to cut it down or not run it at all.

In the case of magazines, sometimes articles are cut regardless of the requested length. In fact, often the editor will assign a longer piece just in case ads don't come in. If the ads come in, your words go out. Don't take it personally.

To add up the number of words, figure each double-spaced computer-written page has between 200–250 words. So, if it's a 1000-word article, it is approximately five manuscript pages. If an editor tells you they want an article that will fill three magazine pages, pin them down on the number of words.

3. *Fact-check your work*

Travel articles and books are loaded with facts and details. Before handing in any manuscript, double check that everything is accurate. If you're not sure about a telephone number, call it or find it listed in at least two—preferably three—other sources.

4. *Edit your work*

Once you complete a work, it's important to go back carefully and edit it to the best of your ability.

5. *Meet all deadlines*

Travel writing is a highly competitive field. If your work is good and always on time, you will please your editors—even if the manuscript sits untouched on their desk for weeks. If you take deadlines lightly, you're doing yourself a big disservice. Even though many editors will set phony deadlines to insure the copy is in on time, your job is to deliver according to the date you agreed on. If an editor doesn't give an exact date (you may hear something like "just get it to me in March," or "as long as I have it by the end of the summer," or "as soon as you can get to it."), insist on one. Deadlines force us to concentrate.

5. *Attach a note to manuscript*

Attach a cover note letting the editor know when you can be reached. If you are going to be traveling, let them know that as well.

6. *Keep a copy of your manuscript as well as all research material*

Once you've submitted your work, it is not necessarily over. Often an editor will call with questions, request more information, or to verify facts. Always have the manuscript (and research material) handy.

Watch Your Words

When writing anything for publication, it's important to avoid using sexist words. Here are some suitable substitutes:

Cowboy	Cow keeper
Caveman	Cave dwellers
First Lady	President's spouse
Forefather	Foreparent
Man-made	Synthetic
Snowman	Snow person
Waitress	Wait person

13.3 Be as Professional as Possible

Many freelance writers choose the profession so they can live an unconventional lifestyle. However, to really make a living as a travel writer, you must treat it as a business and be available to other professionals. Try to:

1. *Set office hours*

Most publishers work Monday through Friday, 9 A.M.–5 P.M. If they're going to call, generally it will be during those times. Get in the habit of being available during those hours or at least some of them. If you're going to be away on trips or just out afternoons, consider calling your machine for messages so you can return calls as soon as possible.

2. *Answer the phone with your name*

Every time I pick up my business phone, I automatically say "Hello, Susan Farewell." It not only sounds professional, but is a repeated affirmation that you are somebody. Do not allow children to answer your business phone unless they have been carefully instructed on how to take messages.

3. *Keep your answering machine announcement professional*

Though you would love to have Eric Clapton blasting out a tune in the background, for your business phone, stick to something simple. Of course, you can be creative, just don't get carried away.

13.4 Write Every Day

Sometimes you'll be so busy with assignments, you'll have no choice but to write every day. But there are plenty of times in a travel writer's career when they are either between assignments or doing research, publicity, or bookkeeping, and not necessarily writing. In order to keep your writing muscles toned, try to write a little each day, even if it's just in your journal. The further you let yourself get away from writing, the harder it is to get back into it. Perhaps the best reason to write every day, however, is to become a great writer. It's very simple: the more you write, the better a writer you become.

13.5 Take Care of Yourself

As I pointed out in Chapter 1, being a self-employed travel writer is an enormously demanding profession that not only requires great discipline, creativity, confidence, enthusiasm, and perseverance but extremely high-energy as well. In order to compete with the best, you have to keep up your health—physically, mentally, and spiritually. In addition to eating three balanced meals a day and getting enough sleep every night, consider the following:

1. *Watch your caffeine and sugar intake*

When working in a home-office, there can be a great temptation to drink coffee and snack through the day. These can affect your moods and energy levels considerably.

2. *Keep alcohol consumption to a minimum or cut out completely*

If you're prone to late-night partying and hangovers, you will have a tough time supporting yourself as a writer. As a travel writer, you will find alcohol flows freely at press events and on press trips.

3. *Exercise regularly*

Sometimes writers get so caught up in projects that the only exercise they get is walking down the stairs—or the driveway—to the mailbox. Make a commitment to yourself to exercise regularly. You might even consider a social sport—such as tennis or basketball—where others will expect you. That way, you have an obligation that must be met.

4. *Take time out*

One of the hazards of working out of your home is a tendency to work around the clock. While other people are out at picnics and football games, you may find yourself sending out tear sheets, invoices, writing or editing. Build into every day time that is totally for you and not related to work in anyway. This can be spent watching a film or TV, reading a novel, playing an instrument, playing with your children or pets, meditating, meeting with friends—what have you. And take complete days off—complete weekends if you're really strong.

5. *Let go of expectations*

Every now and then, you might hear that you're being considered to write something, only to have it fall through. The object is to structure your business so that you constantly have a work in progress, proposals in circulation, and periodic offers, so you will not depend on any one project. This is as much for your peace of mind as for your bank account.

Part Five

DIVERSIFYING YOUR ASSIGNMENTS

CHAPTER
14

Magazines and Newspapers

14.1 Travel Editorials

Writing an editorial can mean anything from writing a 100-word vignette to writing the cover story of a magazine. It can mean writing about one destination, about many destinations, about an aspect of one destination, or a number of other combinations.

Two very popular formats of travel articles are destination pieces and roundups. Destination pieces generally are designed to provide a sense of place about one featured location, along with information on what to see and do, where to shop, where to eat, where to stay, and how to obtain more information. The object is to get all the information in, yet not sound like a laundry list or a guidebook. Sometimes service information (such as telephone numbers, addresses, and prices) is boxed off and put at the end or in a sidebar. Here are some sample destination pieces:

Example #1: Destination piece for Discovery *magazine*

BARBADOS: PARADISE FOUND
by Susan Farewell

It was 6:30 P.M. on the dot when the phone rang.

"Hello madame, this is Winston, your taxi driver from yesterday. Will you be needing a taxi tonight?"

Winston had driven me to a restaurant the night before and offered to call and see if I'd need a ride the following evening. I was astounded when he actually did. He wasn't hired by the hotel. I didn't give him a huge tip the night before. He had no idea that I was writing an article about the island. From what I could tell, there certainly were enough passengers to keep taxi drivers busy.

As I climbed into Winston's spic-and-span taxi half an hour later, I thought, "How can I ever go back to reality?"

Barbados has that affect on almost all its visitors. Blessed with a west coast that's lapped by gentle washes of silky blue sea, a rugged east coast crashed by Atlantic waves, and miles and miles of shimmering cane fields, lush green rain forests, and craggy highlands inland, it's one of the Caribbean's most diversely beautiful islands. It's also one of its most affordable. Though it does have its share of stratospherically-priced resorts, there are more than enough reasonably-priced hotel rooms to go around. The local people are what most visitors remember most, however. They are delightfully friendly.

"Bajans [a nickname for Barbadians] are just plain nice and very reliable people," says Margaret Leacock, a year-round resident originally from England. If anyone knows Barbados and its residents, it's Leacock. She and her husband Jack, one of the island's leading surgeons, have lived on the island for more than thirty years. Leacock runs a small Barbadian enterprise called Custom Tours in which she takes visitors around on personalized tours of Barbados. I asked her whether there was some special be-nice-to-tourists training school that everyone on the island that came in contact with tourists would have to attend. "No," she replied, "Bajans just like people. They're people-watchers. In fact, that's why they build their houses facing the road rather than the sea, so they can watch everyone that passes by."

You won't be on the island more than two minutes before that'll be obvious. Every Bajan you come in contact with at the airport—whether it's the currency exchange cashier, the Barbados Board of Tourism attendant, or one of the luggage handlers—greets you with a smile, a big hello, and often, a "Welcome to Barbados!" I later asked Keithroy (a young student who sat next to me on the bus) why Barbadians are so friendly. "Ma'am" he answered, "we believe visitors are to be treated as special guests. We're flattered that they chose to come visit our island."

It sure is nice to go someplace and be treated like royalty, for a change. All too often, travelers have to fend for themselves. Not on Barbados. On this island, taxi drivers open doors. They offer to wait at the restaurant while you have dinner. At hotels, there are dozens of little touches like hibiscus blossoms thoughtfully arranged on your pillows and the morning paper delivered to your door.

Perhaps the most appealing feature of Barbados, however, is that it's not an island that only the super-rich can afford to visit. Many of the hotels have apartments or suites complete with kitchens or kitchenettes (which means you don't have to eat out all the time), and pull-out sofas if you want to double up with family members or friends. A very attractive two-bedroom suite, suitable for up to four occupants in a south coast hotel, can run about $190 (up until December 15 when prices rise for the winter tourist season) a night. More than two dozen tour operators offer packages where a five-night stay in a leading hotel for two people (including airfare, transfers, hotel, taxes, and service charges—up to December 15) costs as low as $1044. Add another $35–$40 per person, per day for meals.

For 350 years, this small island (21 miles long by 14 across at its widest point) lived and flourished under the British crown, until 1966 when it became a fully independent Commonwealth nation. Today, traces of the mother country are all over. In Bridgetown (the island's commercial and political hub), a bronze statue of Lord Nelson stands in Trafalgar Square (Nelson was stationed in the West Indies for many years). The House of Assembly, north of the square, has stained glass windows representing the English monarchs from James I to Victoria. But it's more than architecture. You can detect a bit of old Shakespearean English in the modern Barbadian dialect (when I asked Keithroy where he lived, he pointed and said, "O'er yonder."). Many resorts serve high tea complete with freshly baked scones, Devonshire cream, and jam. And, vehicles drive on the left side of the road.

At the same time, however, Barbados has a very strong identity of its own and a sense of national pride that makes it one of the most rewarding Caribbean islands to visit. Most Bajans feel there's no place they'd rather be.

There are several restaurants that specialize in local Bajan cuisine as well as those that serve more international dishes. Two of the island's favorite Bajan restaurants are Witch Doctor and Brown Sugar—both have been fixtures on the island for years. As far as other restaurants are concerned, you'll find everyone seems to have his or her own favorite. La Cage aux Folles, Reid's, and Raffles are three reliably good choices. "Though most Bajans have traditionally dined at home, more and more have started to eat out, so the standards of dining have been getting higher and higher," explains Margaret Leacock. "Today, there are several exceptionally good restaurants. Many of the chefs get their experience abroad and return to Barbados, using local cooks and products. The result is very favorable." On menus all over, you'll see flying fish, the national dish. It can be grilled, deep fried, stewed or stuffed and is wonderfully delicate and moist. You'll also find other fresh seafood and fish such as dolphin (sometimes listed on menus as mahi mahi), red snapper, king fish, lobster, crab, and a rare delicacy called sea egg (a kind of sea urchin). The golden meat inside the shell is either fried or steamed, and is available from September to December. Peas and rice is the most common side dish (it's exactly as it sounds, peas—either black-eyed, green peas or lentils—mixed with rice). Pepperpot (a spicy concoction of oxtail, pork, lamb, and chicken) is also a popular dish. Accompanying every meal is a selection of local vegetables like breadfruit which can be pickled with cucumber and spices, or stuffed and baked; the Barbados sweet potato and yam; white eddoes; okras and cassava. There's also a wonderful variety of fruits—bananas, figs, avocado pears, soursop, guavas, paw-paw (papayas), mangoes and coconuts—that are sometimes mixed up in salads and spiced with rum.

Getting around Barbados can be a bit tricky at times, though the roads are generally well maintained, and reasonably well marked. With trucks piled high with sugar cane, confused American tourists, and donkey carts rolling along, it can be a bit of an obstacle course. A great way to explore is in a rented Mini-Moke which looks like a Jeep that never quite grew to full size. They're open-aired, easy to drive and one of the island's most economical buys (about $35–40 US per day). When you're exploring, take your time. The tempo of life is slow here.

Wherever you wander, you're sure to pass miles of cane fields rippling in the soft trade winds. Sugar is the chief export on Barbados and has been since the mid 1600s. Its production ushered in the plantation system that prompted the English to buy thousands of African slaves which is why today the island is 90 percent black. Two working plantations—Francia House and St. Nicholas Abbey—are open to the public for touring.

Though Barbados is blessed with beautiful beaches, it's not just an island of palm trees and sand. In fact, the list of attractions is extraordinarily long. Of course, no one wants to clutter a vacation with too much sightseeing (after all, a vacation means you should relax), but do yourself a favor and spend at least one day touring the island. Here's one tried-and-true itinerary you can easily drive on your own. It takes you along the resort-lined west coast, and the rugged east coast where cliffs drop precipitously into the swirling surf (Margaret Leacock puts it beautifully: "The east coast scenery refreshes the soul."). It passes through cane fields, rain forests, and the northern highlands dotted with grand old British villas, ruins of sugar mills, and candy-colored houses propped up on boulder foundations.

From Bridgetown, head north on Highway 1 along the coast to make a clockwise tour of the island. Your first stop will be Holetown, originally called James Town, where the British landed in 1627 on the ship *Olive Blossom.* Besides an obelisk that marks the spot, there's not a whole lot to see. Be aware, the plaque says they landed in 1605, not 1627 (just a tiny mistake every tour guide will surely point out). Just north of Holetown, you'll pass St. James Church (it dates back to 1875), and a string of luxury hotels and posh private homes including those of Claudette Colbert and assorted British peers. From there, you'll enter busy little Speightstown, once a whaling port, now a fishing town, crowded with shops and people. Just north of Speightstown (around Six Men's Bay and beyond), you can watch skilled craftsmen repair, build and paint the wooden fishing boats you see in waters all around the island. From there, make your way to the Animal Flower Cave on the northernmost tip (natural grottos and sea pools filled with sea anenomes) or cross the island and stop at the Barbados Wildlife Reserve (here, the residents—including turtles, peacocks, and green monkeys—wander freely) and St. Nicholas Abbey (a Jacobean Great House). Cherry Tree Hill is the next stop. Here, you won't be able to take your eyes off the view. In the distance, the Atlantic whips against the shore dramatically. In the foreground, the velvety-green hills of the island's Scotland District spread out before you. Carry on to the Morgan Lewis Mill, the island's only fully intact mill.

At the bottom of the hill, you'll be on the East Coast Highway, a spectacularly scenic road that runs along the ocean. Don't even think about swimming here. The undertow is extremely dangerous. Meander along to Bathsheba, a little fishing village with gigantic waves that attract surfers from around the world, and Tent Bay, where colorful boats bob in the swelling surf. Next stop should be Andromeda Gardens, named after the Greek maiden who was chained to a rock. She had angered Poseidon by saying that her daughters were more beautiful than the nereids (one of whom was Poseidon's wife), and so, he punished her by chaining her to a rock. The gardens are filled with orchids, many of which grow on rocks. Just beyond, St. John's Church is famed for its view and the tomb of Fernando Paleologus, here revered as Constantine's last descendant. To the south stands Codrington College, an active seminary with a long avenue of long-trunked palms. Further south, you'll find Sam Lord's Castle, an opulent mansion in the center of what are now the grounds of the Marriott Resort. Sam Lord was a deplorable character who is said to have lured ships onto the nearby reefs and looted them. From Sam Lord's, head inland to visit Sunbury Plantation House, a 1660 planter's house open for touring. To complete your island loop, head to Oistins on the south coast and follow the coast-road back to your hotel.

Another day, consider heading inland to visit Harrison's Cave (visitors pile into open-aired trains and chug through the subterranean passages by bubbling streams, thundering waterfalls and deep icy pools); the Flower Forest (where you can see soursop, breadfruit and all sorts of other tropical plants); and Francia House, a working plantation house with three roped-off rooms full of antiques.

Plan to spend a morning in Bridgetown, if you want to get some shopping done. Many hotels provide jitney service for their city-bound guests. For the lethargic beachcomber, entering town may come as a bit of a jolt. It (and the rest of the southwest coast) is home to a good chunk of the island's population (260,000). The streets are always busy with shoppers, tourists, business people, and vendors selling everything from slices of freshly-chopped coconut to plastic sandals. Broad Street is the shopping district. You may find that Cave Shepherd (the island's big department store) has everything on your list (rums, crystal, china). The Best of Barbados shop sells wonderful hand-made crafts (pot holders, wood-carved boats, rag dolls) and watercolors by local artist Jill Walker. From town, you can take a bus or taxi to the Garrison Savannah for a walk around the Barbados Museum which has a conscientiously-assembled collection of Barbadian artifacts.

In addition to feasting on spicy island dishes, touring the island's multitude of sights, and lazing days away on sun-saturated beaches, you'll find the sports scene on Barbados first rate. There are three golf courses (an 18-hole course at Sandy Lane, and two nine-hole courses at Rockley Resort Hotel and Heywoods Resort Hotel), four riding stables offering rides through sugar cane fields and along sandy beaches (Brighton Stables 425–9381; Country Corral Riding Stables 422–2401; Valley Hill Stables 423–0033; Ye Olde Congo Road Stables 423–6180), and dozens of tennis courts (just about all the hotels have some). There's also snorkeling and scuba diving (Folkestone Underwater Park on the west coast has a specially marked marine trail), and sailing on the calm Caribbean west coast, and surfing on the east coast.

If you'd rather sit back and observe, you can watch a cricket game (fall is a good time for this), a hockey game, or the Barbados International Surfing Championship (in November).

In the evenings, two boat companies offer dinner cruises. *The Bajan Queen*, a Mississippi-style riverboat and *The Jolly Roger*, a sailboat. Both offer calypso music, Bajan buffet dinners, and dancing for about $40–45 US per person. There are also two dinner productions worth taking in. Staged in the courtyard of the Barbados Museum, *1627 And All That* is a marvelous extravaganza of dancing and singing combined with a traditional Bajan buffet (about $35 US per person). *Barbados, Barbados* is a musical comedy based on the life of Rachel Pringle, one of the island's true characters at Balls Sugar Plantation (about $35 US per person).

By the end of your visit to Barbados, you'll not only be tan, but mentally stimulated (you can't help but want to find out more about the West Indies), perhaps in better shape (that is, if you take advantage of the sports scene), well-fed, relaxed, happy, and probably spoiled for life. No more Winstons at your beck and call.

(sidebar)

Best Barbados Bets

Homes Away from Home

You'll find the biggest concentration of reasonably priced hotels along the south coast of the island. Some of the most popular include the Divi Southwinds Beach Hotel (until mid-December, double rooms start at about $120 a night; a two-bedroom suite—suitable for four occupants—runs about $190); Southern Palms (up to December 15, twin bedrooms run $98 a night; suites with balconies, kitchenettes, and ocean views cost $150); Casuarina Beach Club (pool or garden view double rooms start at $90; one-bedroom suites go for $110). Over on the southeast coast, is Ginger Bay Beach Club, where double rooms costs $105 a day off season, and $180 during peak season (that's after December 15). You'll find almost all Barbadian hotel rooms have terraces or patios, a lot of space to spread out in, kitchenettes or mini bars, ceiling fans and/or air conditioning.

The west coast is lined with one luxury hotel after another, including The Royal Pavilion, Glitter Bay, Sandy Lane, Coral Reef, Cobblers Cove, and Treasure Beach. For the most part, double rooms start in the neighborhood of $150–200 during summer months, and soar up to $250, $300 in winter. If you're willing to splurge, it's worth it. These properties are nonpareil.

Bajan Bites

For possibly the best local meal to be had, make a point of going to Shirley's, an open-aired, beach-front restaurant in Speightstown. Though the decor is budget (the concrete floor slants a bit, the tables are cheap vinyl/metal numbers, the lightbulb shades are rusted tin cans), the food is unfailingly good. For less than $10 per person, you get a home-cooked Bajan meal—usually it's fried chicken, beef stew or a fish dish (flying fish, king fish or dolphin) accompanied by peas and rice, cou-cou, a salad, pickled beets and breadfruit. Two other Bajan restaurants include Witch Doctor (428–7856) and Brown Sugar (426–7684). Both are more geared-for-tourists as far as decor and prices go (dinners cost at least $18–25 per person).

For a special dinner (read: expensive, but worth it), consider La Cage Aux Folles (432–1203), where the dishes look like they should be on the cover of *Gourmet* magazine (try the Chicken Tandori which arrives in a sea of sauce, topped with a nest of sprouts, sliced cucumbers and Chinese vegetables). A four-course meal for two at this west coast restaurant costs about $80–$90 US (not including wine). Also on the west coast is Reid's (432–7623) where you dine amid a profusion of palms and flowers, with a symphony of tree frogs all around. Dishes like Dover Sole Rockefeller and Dolphin Fricassee along with a delicious array of appetizers and homemade desserts add up to at least $60 for two (not including liquor). In Holetown, you'll find Raffles (432–1280), housed in a former chattel house. Absolutely every detail here is a conversation piece—from the ebony African napkin holders to the check, which comes in a basket of fragrant blossoms. The food—blackened dolphin, curried chicken, peppercorn lamb (just to name a few main dishes)—is astonishingly good. Expect to spend at least $100 for two (plus wine).

Coming Attractions

During the month of August, you can get tickets for Barbados Best on Stage. It's a series of dance, music, and comedy performances at Frank Collymore Hall in Bridgetown. Contact the tourism office for the various locations of the Sir Garfield Sobers International Schools Cricket Tournament which takes place July 16–August 6, and the Banks Barbados International Hockey Festival (August 19–25). During October and November, there will be several competitions and performances in dance, drama, singing, acting, and writing as part of the National Independence Festival of Creative Arts. The Barbados International Surfing Championship is held at the Soup Bowl on the east coast November 2–4. In early December (the first and second of the month), several foot races take place as part of the Run Barbados Series.

For more information, contact the Barbados Board of Tourism. In New York, 800 Second Avenue, New York, NY 10017; (800) 221–9831, (212) 986–6516. In California, 3440 Wilshire Boulevard, Suite 1215, Los Angeles, CA 90010; (213) 380–2198.

Example #2: Destination piece for The New York Post

MARGARITA ISLAND: A CARIBBEAN STEAL
by Susan Farewell

Sorry gang, but you can't get a margarita on Margarita Island. The island doesn't import tequila. In fact, the name has nothing to do with the Mexican drink. Still, it's an island guaranteed to give you a buzz with its super-friendly people, its sun-bleached beaches, its duty-free bargains, and its jaw-droppingly low prices. And besides, Margarita Island's pink rum punches blow the average margarita right out off the bar.

You're not alone if you have to look at a map to figure out where it is. Most North Americans have never even heard of Margarita Island. Actually, it's two land masses connected by an isthmus, about 20 miles north of the Venezuelan mainland. That's about as south as you can go in the Caribbean Sea. Sound like it would take days to get to? Relax. You'll just be settling in for a cat nap after a meal on the plane and before you know it, the seatbelt light will ding on, and the pilot will be instructing the flight attendants to prepare for landing. You can fly direct from New York in four and a half hours or take a flight that connects in Caracas, adding another 35 minutes to the trip.

Some say beaches are Margarita's biggest draw. They come

in all sizes, shapes, and styles including the isolated, no-sign-of-other-people type to the let's-party, spirited Rio variety backed by open-aired seafood restaurants and thatch-roofed bars. Though there are *playas* around the port of Porlamar on the southeast coast (where the biggest concentration of hotels and tourist facilities are concentrated), it's worth renting a car (about a fourth of what you pay back home) to explore the 40-odd other beaches that frame the island.

You'll find the most popular strands on the northeastern shores, all clearly indicated on the tourist map (free at hotels) by an illustration of a beach umbrella. (By the way, *use* umbrellas. This close to the equator, the sun's rays are alarmingly strong). Among the favorites are Playa Guacucu, Punta Cardon, Playa El Tirano, El Agua and Manzanillo—all mattress-soft sweeps of beach with powerful surfs. Caraqueños (residents of Caracas) and other Venezuelans flock to these beaches weekends and holidays, showing up in every kind of bathing suit imaginable. Most fun is parking yourselves at a beach restaurant where you can squeeze lemon onto a pile of fresh shrimp or *langosta* (lobster) and take quenching swigs of a chilled Polar (Venezuelan beer) while you watch the whole carnival-like scene.

Other beaches to keep an eye out for are those near the village of Pedro Gonzales (there's a still-water and an ocean beach) and the long white ocean beach at Juangriego.

The island's most famous beach is at La Restinga, a barrier reef that connects Margarita Island with Peninsula de Macanao, its western part. To reach it, you take a motorboat ride from Porlamar (about $4 each) that whizzes you over to a maze of mangrove trees rising out of a lagoon. As you skim through the tangled greens, keep your eyes open for a long-legged scarlet ibis. This is one of its few habitats in the world. You might also spot some hawks (on winter leave from the north) and pelicans doing their jet-like take-offs and dive-bomb fishing routines.

If you're looking to spread your towels on a footprint-less strand, you'll have your choice of spots on the Macanao Peninsula. Follow the road to Punta Avenas on the westernmost point if you really want to get away from it all.

While some visitors maintain that beaches are Margarita Island's biggest forte, others rave on more about the shopping. In fact, most devote at least a day or two in Porlamar (the island's tourism and commercial hub) combing the shops that sell everything from Obsession perfume to Ralph Lauren silk bathrobes duty free. Since 1975, Margarita Island has been a free port, attracting throngs of Venezuelans who flock to the island as New Yorkers do to 14th Street to save as much as 50 percent on clothes, jewelry, and other personal items. North Americans and other visitors from abroad have the added advantage of the exchange rate which at press time is 42 Bolivares to the dollar and still dropping. Years ago—when Venezuela was its most prosperous—it was three Bolivares to the dollar. Do yourselves an enormous favor though and check the at-home prices before uncrumpling those Monopoly-like bills. Not all merchandise prices are that good a bargain to begin with.

Aside from miles of sun-bleached beaches and scores of duty-free shops, Margarita has some interesting colonial towns and forts to see. If time is limited, at least make your way to La Asunción, the island's colonial capital. Tucked away in the green pointed inland hills and guarded by the Santa Rosa fortress, it has an open-air museum-like quality with its faded pastel buildings, its ornate iron work and centuries-old walls. The convent, the church, the stone bridge, the sun dial, and what is now the Nueva Cadiz

Museum (it used to be the seat of government and later a jail), all date back to the 16th and 17th centuries.

Another town to make time for is the deep-water port of Pampatar, which is largely dominated by its fort. Its crisp white colonial church and white-washed buildings crowned by red-tile rooftops look like something you'd find in the Spanish countryside. You really shouldn't miss the village of Juangriego either. This is Margarita Island's other up-and-coming tourist town, also home to a fort. Plan to be in the area around sunset; every day it's an applaudable extravaganza.

Back in Porlamar, there are several very good and inexpensive restaurants to try including El Bahia (Av. Raul Leoni Via El Morro; Tel: 614556), an enormously popular Spanish dinner spot. This is a good place to try *pabellón criolla* (Venezuela's national dish), a spicy stew of shredded beef, black beans, cheese, egg, white rice, and fried plantains. Entrees run from $3–$7. Another good bet is Da Gaspar (Av. 4 de Mayo; Tel: 613486), a seafood restaurant with some German dishes. The lobster here is deliriously good. Several other cuisines are represented in Porlamar as well, including French, Italian, and Chinese.

After a satiating meal, you can take your pick of after-dark spots including a handful of discos (Doce 34 on Av. 4 de Mayo is the current hot spot) and piano bars at the big hotels.

Whether you choose Margarita Island for the beaches, the duty-free shopping, the food, or the people, you can't go wrong with the price. Ask your travel agent about air/hotel packages that start as low as $599 (taxes and surcharges not included) for seven night stays. They include first-rate accommodations in the island's top hotels such as the brand new Hilton International, right smack-dab on the beach. It has 280 guest rooms, many with sea views and private balconies. Sporting facilities include a huge swimming pool, a gym, sauna, tennis courts, and water sports. There are also two restaurants, a bar, a nightclub, and a full-service business center. With Hilton's new Venezuelan Great Escape package, you can combine a two-day stay at the Caracas Hilton with a five-day stay at the Margarita Hilton, for just $323 per person (includes a welcome drink and free tennis). For more details, call 1-800-HILTONS.

Another package hotel is the Margarita Concorde, related to the Concorde on Aruba. Poised on the shores of El Morro Bay, this 526-room, 24-floor hotel boasts all the amenities of a first-class resort including a pool, a gym, restaurant, and a nightclub.

You can fly direct to Margarita Island from New York on Saturdays or Sundays on Viasa Airlines or fly first to Caracas on Avensa Airlines, Viasa, Pan American or Eastern and connect with the 35-minute Avensa flight over to Margarita. Air fares run between $363–$398 if you decide against one of the package deals.

For more information, contact the Embassy of Venezuela, Information and Cultural Service, 2437 California Street, N.W., Washington, D.C. 20008; (202) 797–3800.

Example #3: Destination piece for Gulliver *magazine (a magazine for Japanese travelers published in Tokyo)*

MAINE: AN AMERICAN PLACE
by Susan Farewell

"That's him in the green shirt!" a middle-aged woman blurted out, shaking with excitement as she ripped her husband's twin-torpedo-like binoculars from around his neck, practically strangling the poor old guy in the process. Bush-watchers are a whole new breed in these parts. Armed with film, they park their cars along cliff-hanging Ocean Avenue and follow the road that passes the presidential compound outside of Kennebunkport as if making their way to Mecca. They travel to this coastal village to see the summer White House, a nine-bedroom shingled house propped up on a beautiful promontory surrounded by the Atlantic Ocean. The house has been in Bush's family since 1903.

These same tourists are usually the ones that are happy with what they first find in Maine: the picturesque fishing villages, the Andrew Wyeth landscapes, the big lobster dinners. Maine attracts a lot of these types, Americans on vacation in search of the picture of Maine they've had since childhood. Over the years, this New England state has practically become synonymous with the word "vacation." In fact, license plates say, "Maine—Vacationland."

Aside from Alaska, Maine is the northernmost state in the United States. About two-thirds of it are bordered by eastern Canada. Quebec and Ottawa are both less than a couple of hours away (by car). Its southern areas (including Bush Country) are within easy reach of Boston (about a two-hour drive) and New York (about five or six-hours).

Maine has its Ice Age to thank for its natural good looks. Massive glaciers left over 6000 lakes and ponds and 32,000 miles of rivers and streams in their wake as well as the towering peaks of Cadillac Mountain and Mt. Katahdin (the latter stretches about a mile high). The coast is made of a series of deeply cut indentations and narrow peninsulas and has more offshore islands than you can count. The name Maine supposedly comes from sailors who used the term main when speaking of the mainland apart from the offshore islands. In later years, Maine was given its nickname—Pine Tree State—because nearly ninety percent of its land is covered with fragrant evergreens.

As with all beautiful places, Maine's beauty was first discovered by artists, then by wealthy families, and later, by tourists. As a result, much of the coastline (especially in the south, since it's most accessible) is dotted with fishing and lobstering towns that have been so gussied up for tourists, they're almost too cute. As one resident put it, "There's a lot of danger in being so picturesque."

The truth is, Maine really doesn't need to do anything to attract people. Like a naturally beautiful woman, she doesn't need makeup. She also doesn't need the endorsement of a president, and most assuredly need not resort to such gimmicky names as Kenne*bush*port and Bush Country, and—shudder—Bush Gardens North.

Real Mainers know this. So do the summer home owners. The latter have bought hunks of ocean-front property and whole islands to assure they'll always have a piece of the unadulterated Maine coast. Many summer families own hand-me-down "cottages," with a maze of bedrooms and bathrooms, that were built in the late 1800s by their great grandparents. These homes are not quite as opulent as the Newport mansions, but are certainly as grand, often with exquisite mahogany woodwork, massive stone fireplaces, and wraparound porches. Some hide behind stands of evergreen trees, others are propped up on hilltops, exposing themselves to the world.

Beautiful though these estates may be, they do, however, have a way of hogging the shoreline. As a result, all too often the average visitor's access to the coast is reduced to admiring it from the deck of a sightseeing boat, from a picnic table in a state park, or from a people-dotted public beach. Though these are not bad alternatives, the real beauty of Maine should be seen and experienced close-up.

Fortunately, there are many hotels and inns along the coast that not only provide unending hospitality and an array of amusements, but open the door to the very soul of Maine. Here are three such places that—though dramatically different in presentation—invite you to discover the truly opiatic affects of this coast, which some choose to call Bush Country. All three are within easy reach of the Presidential compound which is locally known as Walker's Point. If you want to join the scores of Bush-watchers (especially in August, when the president is vacationing) or just get a glimpse of the compound, take a drive along mansion-dotted Ocean Avenue. If the president is in town, you may have to park along the cliffs and walk. It's quite a scene, with a battery of Secret Service agents, the Maine State Police accompanied by German Shepherds, and the media all trying to find an angle on Bush's summer vacation.

An Island for Rent

The experience of having your own summer home in Maine can be simulated (fortunately, without the headaches) by staying at Hope Island, a privately owned 13-bedroom house that has been passed down through the generations of an old New England family. Poised on its own 85-acre island in Casco Bay, Hope Island is surrounded by hundreds of spruce and fir-covered islands that lie off the Portland coast between Cape Elizabeth and Small Point. Though many are privately owned, a handful of them are home to small, intensely interesting communities, some which still make their living from the sea. The waters that slosh between them are filled with bluefish, mackerel, tuna, and seals as well as sailboats and other seagoing vessels. Portland—Maine's most vibrant city—is about half an hour away.

The New England mansion is rented to groups of 10 to 25 people at a time complete with an attentive—though not fawning—staff of seven. Among them is a young and innovative chef, who after years of preparing warm-water fish at a Caribbean resort, is now doing wonders with the local catches. Each day a supply of lobsters is dropped off by a local lobsterman in a submerged box that dangles from the end of the island's dock. The chef will also prepare any fish that guests catch. Dinners—which tend to be dressed-up affairs—are served in the dining room on the original family's china along with antique silver and pressed linens. The most coveted wines and desserts that elicit a whole string of oohs and aahs complete the picture.

The interior of the house is as any good summer Maine home should be: simple, unpretentious, and deliriously comfortable. The centerpiece of it all is an immense living room designed around an immense hearth. On one of the antique tables lies the house guest books—which date back to 1945—filled with fond recollections such as "All alone but I have Hope." The living room opens on to a wide porch overlooking the sea, giving one the distinct feeling of being on a ship. Individual guest rooms are also very simply furnished with brass or iron beds and painted furniture. Some have fireplaces, all have views of the sea and islands all around.

The piney woods that cover the island are punctuated with fern grottos, birch trees, slopes of bayberry and meadows colonized by wildflowers—all of which can be seen by following the well-worn footpaths. You're never more than a minute's walk from the sea which is always astoundingly beautiful whether bundled in mist or reflective as mica. Rocky beaches frame the island giving way to quiet coves and inlets where it's not uncommon to see a great blue heron standing like a caryatid. You can swim if the urge hits. Be forewarned though—Maine water never seems to warm up enough.

If you're feeling ambitious, there's a whole menu of on and off-island diversions to take your pick of, including deep-sea fishing, sailing, water skiing, golf and tennis, and duck hunting in the fall. At any time guests can be shuttled by the island's sea captain to the mainland or neighboring islands including next-door Cliff Island which has a year-round population of forty, a one-room school house, and a tiny wood church—the essence of Maine's charm without the souvenir vendors. Guests can also be taken by boat to the Freeport Landing, be picked up by a L. L. Bean van and let loose in the factory-outlet town of Freeport (by the way, besides its phenomenally successful retail and mail-order business, L. L. Bean offers classes and workshops in everything from fly casting and coastal kayaking in fair-weather months to cross country and telemark skiing in winter).

Perhaps the most unforgettable moment of anyone's stay on Hope Island is falling asleep to the tolling of a bell buoy and the uproarious sea crashing below. As one anonymous poet put it in the house history, "You will never be the same after sleeping on an island."

Hope Island is available for a week or a month at a time from May to November for $150 per person (minimum ten people) per day. That includes three meals daily and use of the boats (sailboat is extra). There is an additional 15 percent service charge, 7 percent Maine tax, and liquor is not included. The rate is slightly higher during duck hunting season. For more information, write: Resorts Management, Inc., The Carriage House at 201½ East 29th Street, New York, NY 10016, or call: (212) 696–4566.

A Grand Old Summer Hotel

Back in the late 1800s when wealthy New Yorkers, Bostonians and other out-of-towners were flocking to the rocky islands and peninsulas of Maine to build their summer houses, the Black Point Inn came into being. Like many of its neighbors—most of which were designed by the Portland architect, John Calvin Stevens—it's a massive shingled-style building complete with a front porch and far-reaching ocean views. The main house has sixty guest rooms and there are another twenty in cottages on the grounds.

Prouts Neck is a small peninsula, jutting opportunistically into Saco Bay about eight miles south of Portland. Much of its coastal scenery—steep cliffs, swirling surf, and dwarfish rock-clinging trees—can be seen on the canvases of the American painter Winslow Homer, who lived and worked there. His studio, a converted stable overlooking the ocean, is open to the public for touring.

Like Hope Island, the Black Point Inn is truly grand, but not pretentious. Rooms are decorated very simply with white crewel bedspreads, crisp white curtains, and rock maple beds. There are no lavish antiques, marble bathrooms, or other Trump-like amenities. The lobby and parlor rooms are functionally furnished with comfortable sofas and the kind of chairs you can flop into.

The common pursuit of all visitors is to relax and absorb the beauty of the surroundings. Each day is bookended by spectacular sunrises and sunsets, both of which can be seen from the inn, thanks to its east-west setting. Between the sun's performances, you may follow Cliff Walk, a narrow footpath that meanders above the coastline, taking you past the subjects of many of Homer's paintings. There are also two beaches to sun on or swim off of and a fleet of boats for rent at the local Yacht Club. Birdwatchers can log in all sorts of interesting sightings at the Prouts Neck Bird Sanctuary and on nearby Bluff and Stratton Islands. For those interested in sports, the Prouts Neck Country Club—open to all inn guests—has an 18-hole golf course and over a dozen tennis courts. And right at the inn, there's an indoor and outdoor pool, two Jacuzzis, and a sauna.

Though the inn prides itself on generous servings of local fish and lobster (you could have lobster every night in some form or another if you cared to), you can count on some other American favorites like grilled steaks and an assortment of veal and chicken dishes.

During the months of July and August, all three meals are included in the room rates. The inn is open from early May to October. Rates range from $105 to $150 per person per night plus the 7 percent Maine hotel tax. For more information, write the Black Point Inn, Prouts Neck, Maine 04074, or call: (207) 883–4126.

A Perfect New England Inn

In-town inns along the coast of Maine have their own set of endearments. They're often surrounded by stately white houses with columned front porches. Their streets and sidewalks are usually busy with salty locals. Many have worthwhile shops and galleries you might miss during a brief day visit. And in most cases, there's at least a couple of days worth of good seafood restaurants within walking distance. Such is the case with The Captain Lord Mansion, a three-story Federal house crowned by a widow's walk in Kennebunkport.

The building itself is a masterpiece, built during the War of 1812 by Captain Lord, a wealthy merchant and ship builder who put his men to work building while the British blockaded Kennebunkport. Inside, it has all the hallmarks of a ship carpenter's craft, including a suspended elliptical staircase, blown-glass windows, and mahogany doors with brass locks. The whole house has been so well preserved over the years that some of the original wallpaper is still intact. Each of the sixteen rooms has been imaginatively decorated with period-reproduction wallpaper, exquisite antiques, and four-poster beds (some are so high, you have to climb up into them). Many have working fireplaces, all have private baths. Instead of rooms numbers, each one is named after a ship built by various members of the Lord family.

Though there's no restaurant at the inn, every morning breakfast is announced by sweet melodies played on a coin-operated symphonion. An important meal for Mainers, it's served family-style in the kitchen on a pair of Harvest tables. There's always an assortment of baked goods (such as banana bread with nuts and oatmeal-jam muffins) still warm from the oven, as well as eggs any way you like them, and fresh yogurt topped with local blueberries.

For other meals, you can take your pick of restaurants in Kennebunkport. Beverly Davis and Rick Litchfield—the innkeepers—get you started with a huge leather portfolio they've stuffed with menus from all over town. On some, they've jotted down their own critiques. Being that you are in the heart of Bush Country in Kennebunkport, you will see notes such as "John was one of fifty-two chefs to prepare food for the inauguration" scribbled here and there.

If you want to dine near the Bush action, try the Shawmut Inn (when the president's in town, usually in August). That's where most of the reporters stay, all trying to look like they're actually working as they feast on spanking fresh fish. Cape Arundel Inn overlooks the presidential compound and serves up a delicious brunch that's seafood-oriented (try the scallops in puff pastry). The Olde Grist Mill has President Bush's approval. A photograph of him is displayed prominently in the entrance along with some praisefull remarks. The view here is overrated (when the tide is out, you find yourselves looking at an enormous mud puddle), but the food—predominately seafood as well—is celestial.

Summer White House or no summer White House, this little town has been on the tourist map of Maine for a long time. It's home to one impeccably preserved historic house after another. There are all sorts of boating excursions from whale watching cruises to deep-sea fishing, as well as biking routes, horseback riding stables, wide open beaches, golf courses, and nature preserves.

The mansion is open twelve months a year. Rates generally run between $100–$175 per room (includes breakfast for two) during the high season, and $85 to $145 between January and April (also includes breakfast for two). Add 7 percent for the Maine hotel tax. For more information, write: The Captain Lord Mansion, P.O. Box 800, Kennebunkport, Maine 04046, or call: (207) 967–3141.

Spring and fall months are among the finest of the Maine year, often with temperatures in the 70s, though summers are traditionally considered the Maine vacation season.

(side bar #1)

State of the Arts

Along with pine trees and lobster, Maine is rife with artists. Not only are there a profusion of galleries and museums tucked away in all sorts of unexpected places, but many studios and workshops are open to the public. Here's a sampling of what you'll find.

Broad Bay Inn and Gallery: In the barn out back, there's a complete gallery of paintings and crafts. Though the inn is open all year, the gallery is only open from the end of June to the end of October, Wednesdays through Sundays or by appointment. Main Street, Waldoboro Village. Tel: (207) 832–6668.

Eastern Bay Cooperative Gallery: In the tiny fishing village of Stonington on Deer Isle (which is connected to the mainland by a bridge), this cooperative gallery showcases the works of over fifty Maine craftspeople and artists. On Main Street. Tel: (207) 367–5006 (hours vary).

Haystack Mountain School of Crafts: At the end of a bumpy dirt road on Deer Isle, you'll find this crafts school where artists from around the world gather to produce works in metal, textiles, wood, glass, pottery, and paper in a series of studios designed by noted architect Edward Larrabee Barnes. None of the works are for sale at the school, but many are available at various studios and galleries around the island including the Blue Heron Gallery and Studio in Deer Isle Village. Haystack is open between June and early September, 10 A.M. to 4 P.M. Free tours are conducted daily at 1 P.M. Route 15. Tel: (207) 348–2306.

Jud Hartman Gallery and Sculpture Studio: A self-taught artist, Jud Hartman has created a series of bronze sculptures depicting the Amerindians of the Northeast. In addition, there's a changing exhibit of watercolor paintings. On Main Street in Blue Hill. Tel: (207) 374–9917. Open all year, 10 A.M.–5 P.M.

Leighton Gallery: Works by over thirty contemporary Maine artists are changed monthly in this well-known gallery. There's also a sculpture garden. Parker Point Road, Blue Hill. Tel: (207) 374–5001.

Maine Coast Artists: A nonprofit gallery dedicated to promoting contemporary Maine art. On Russell avenue in Rockport's historic firehouse. Tel: (207) 236–2875.

Maine Potters's Market: A cooperative gallery featuring the works of fifteen local potters. In Portland's Old Port District, 376 Fore Street, Portland. Tel: (207) 774–1633.

Portland Museum of Art: A striking postmodern building designed by Henry N. Cobb of I. M. Pei, the city's most prominent museum houses extensive collections of Maine-based artists such as Andrew Wyeth, Edward Hopper, and Winslow Homer. It's open Tuesday-Saturday, 10–5 and on Thursdays to 9 P.M. and Sunday noon to 5 P.M. 7 Congress Square, Portland. Tel: (207) 773–2787.

Ronald Hayes Pearson: Exquisite silver and gold jewelry is displayed at the artist's gallery and workshop on Old Ferry Road on Deer Isle. Call for hours, (207) 348–2535.

Six Clay Artists: A cooperative gallery shared by six artists. 131 Sawyer Street, South Portland. Tel: (207) 767–7113.

The Dancing Blanket: Handwoven blankets, clothing, and accessories by Cynthia McGuirl are the *specialite de la maison* here. Custom orders are welcome. The studio is located on Route 131, about eight miles from Route 1 in Thomaston. Tel: (207) 373–8625.

The Eastport Gallery: As one local artist put it, "All great places are discovered—or rediscovered—by artists." Such is the case with this former sardine canning town on the northernmost coast of Maine. Here, the painters and potters are the prominent citizens, their works on display in a converted warehouse building at 51–53 Dana Street in Eastport. Tel: (207) 853–4166.

The Rockport Apprenticeshop: The art of building wooden boats is still very much alive in the state of Maine. Visitors can tour workshops and exhibits and browse around the store. Sea Street, Rockport. Tel: (207) 236–6071.

(sidebar #2)

Maineana

There's no question. Maine has a lot of character. You can see it everywhere—from the flurry of whirligigs (wooden flapping ducks, paddling fisherman, trotting horses) that decorate front lawns to the profusion of businesses named for their owners (Larry's Lobster, Amy's Place, Ray's Meat Market). For a real close-up look at this state's folk culture, consider making your way to the following.

Yard Sales: Sundays—during the late summer and autumn months—is when many Mainers drag out dusty old ping-pong tables or folding tables and pile them high with used dishes, irons, rusty tools, and anything else they think they can sell. They usually set everything out in driveways along with a couple of lawn chairs for themselves and any passersby who want to settle in for awhile. A hand-printed sign—whether it reads Garage Sale, Tag Sale, Yard Sale, Moving Sale, or Two-Family House Sale—gets nailed to the nearest telephone pole. Some families put an ad in the local papers a couple of days before. Then comes the wait. A patient wait for the occasional pick-up truck or out-of-town license-plated car to drive up for a look around. Many State-of-Mainers make a day of shopping at these sales, checking off ads in classified sections as they go along.

For many, this is a chance to visit with neighbors and swap a gossip or two. Though you're not likely to find valuable antiques at these places, you may walk away with something truly Americana like a stuffed Garfield that, who knows, someday might be valuable. You can find these yard sales all over Maine, just look for the signs.

Flea Markets: Flea Markets are a variation of the aforementioned yard sale. They're bigger affairs, attracting hundreds of dealers who display their collections on long tables set up end to end in fields or parking lots. These are professionals, spending part of their week buying, the other part selling.

One of the state's biggest is the Montsweagg Flea Market in Woolwich, Maine, right off Route One, on the way up to some of the state's most popular coastal resort areas. You'll find everything from old postcards to used lawn mowers. Occasionally something valuable is unearthed.

Bingo Games: Bingo is a passion among many Mainers, especially in the more rural areas. All over the state, you'll see signs outside fire houses and community centers announcing "Bingo, tonight at 8" or "Bingo every Wednesday." You're welcome to pull up and join in. For a small charge at the door and for each card you play, you can compete with the old pros who quietly listen as the leader twirls a wire ball filled with numbered cubs and calls out the various numbers. The lucky one to fill five spaces in a row on their card (horizontally, vertically, or diagonally) yells out triumphantly "BINGO!" and can walk away with as much as $25,000 in jackpot money. Most fun is observing the players who clench their good-luck charms, cross their fingers, and pray they'll win.

Country Fairs: Colorful banners stretched across the Main Streets of small towns all over Maine make it virtually impossible to miss these events. Often the town's whole population participates in some form or other, whether by baking apple pies for the bake sale, knitting pot holders for the arts and crafts table, or donating used books and clothes for the second-hand shop. Some offer pony rides, Dunk the Maiden, and other amusements for children.

Roundups generally include several various destinations, such as the following:

Example #1: A roundup of hotels for Child *magazine*

GOING OUR WAY: TRAVELING WITH CHILDREN
by Susan Farewell

Remember the game where you'd close your eyes, spin a globe, and let your finger slide until it stopped rotating?

Wherever you were pointing when it bumped to a halt—whether it was some unpronounceable city in Singapore or a pea of an island in the Baltic Sea—was where you were destined to go. You either lucked out or got stuck with some "weird" country. "Oh well," you said. "It was just for fun anyway."

Nowadays, kids go to these places. All over the world, there are hotels and resorts in truly grand or remote settings that have a real soft spot for the short-set as well as a complete understanding of parents in need of all-out pampering. On the following pages, we've selected five top-drawer hotels that go beyond the obligatory dining room high chairs and skimpily-stocked game rooms. These places treat children as esteemed guests and offer delightful diversions such as bush walking in Australia and skating lessons in Switzerland. Each one has babysitting services and/or full-time nannies. And of course, when the need for a bottle to be warmed or carrots to be pureed comes up, you won't see a horrified waiter whisper to a maitre d' and then disappear for half an hour. On top of all that, for parents, these hotels are—quite simply—the *creme de la creme.* Guess it's time to dust off the globe . . .

Go For It: The Great Barrier Reef

Hayman Resort, Hayman Island, Australia

"The Great Barrier Reef was always on our 'Someday List,' " explained Ann, a Princeton-based art teacher. "We never even considered going now, especially with 5-year-old Charlotte still dragging her 'cwa-vah' (translation: cover) wherever she goes." That was until her husband Mike, a partner in an architectural firm, brought home a brochure from a colleague who had spent a week at a Down Under resort with his wife and kids. "One look at the photographs and we were sold," Ann explained. "We couldn't decide what was more beautiful, the sea and mountains looming in the distance or the geometrically shaped pools stretching off in every direction." She continued, "The real clincher though was that Mike said his associate raved about the kid's activities program as much as he did the diving!"

"Once we got there, we knew why. We'd come back from a day of snorkeling and our eight-year-old son Dustin would be talking a mile a minute about how he made billy tea and damper over a fire. He'd use all sorts of Aussie phrases as he'd tell us stories about bushwalking to the Lookout. Of course, Charlotte went too, but couldn't get a word in edgewise." The program of kid's activities at Hayman Island keeps five to fifteen-year-olds going from 9 to 9 daily (10–4 on Tuesdays and Sundays). While you're out paddling about in a hauntingly beautiful and completely silent submarine world, they might be riding ponies through a rain forest, digging for treasures on a beach, or also pollywogging around in masks and fins (with helpful instructors at their sides). There are barbecues, arts and crafts sessions, face painting contests, scavenger hunts, Newcombe ball games (like volleyball, but easier for little kids), and a wacky selection of pool games like diving for spoons and torpedoing through underwater hoops, plus a long list of water sports including paddleboarding, waterskiing, and board sailing. After dinner, diversions include trivial pursuit challenges, bingo games, and videos. For children under five, there's a day nursery and 24-hour baby sitting service.

The regal Hayman Resort propped on an island of the same name in the WhitSunday Islands was recently reopened after an ambitious redevelopment program that transformed it from a mediocre hotel to a grand, ultra-luxurious resort where nothing short of "the best" would fit in. The setting alone transcends your wildest South Pacific dreams with the sea—a carpet of blues and greens—sloshing against sandy beaches that look as though they were washed in chlorine bleach. The grounds are artfully landscaped with hundreds of palm trees and explosively fragrant gardens. There's a Japanese garden fashioned after those at the Katsun Place in Japan complete with a waterfall, rock pool, and stone lanterns. Inside is even more artistic with a multimillion-dollar collection of paintings, sculpture, tapestries, vases and other objets d'art by well-known Australian artists throughout the public areas and guest rooms. All guest rooms have private balconies or patios and views of the Whitsunday passage, the pools, and gardens. They're attractively decorated with cane and leather furnishings, handwoven rugs, marble bathrooms, and soft-colored bedspreads and draperies and are roomy enough to spread out kid's "stuff." Each one has a refrigerator and fully stocked bar (the latter on request). Though there are air conditioners and ceiling fans, most guests prefer the tepid breezes off the sea that waft in as though keeping time with a metronome.

Obviously, one of the biggest attractions for grownups at Hayman Island is the Great Barrier Reef, a magic kingdom underwater. You'll find everything from introductory snorkeling lessons to advanced PADI courses in open-water diving, as well as classes in underwater photography, night diving, and coral reef ecology. But you don't have to go snorkeling or diving. In fact, there's a whole host of other water sports at Hayman Island including windsurfing, boating, fishing, sailing, water skiing, and parasailing, plus tennis courts and aerobics facilities.

If you're more interested in all-out relaxing, there's a full-scaled spa where the biggest effort you'll make is going from the sauna to plunge pool and back, or flipping over for the masseuse. After a half day of treatments, you'll walk out feeling as floppy as a ragdoll with a satiated glow. Equally as luxurious is plopping down on chaise longues by the pool. A good novel, an occasional dunk, and a fruity concoction in hand, and you'll be glad "someday" has arrived.

For dining, you'll find five different restaurants serving five different cuisines including French, Polynesian, and Italian. Additionally, there are several bars and lounge areas (including a Billiard Room and Card Room) where you can sit and sip while the children are off having their own dinner with new-found friends. There are also dinner and cocktail cruises where you glide along the Whitsunday Passage, the islands illuminated by a Titanic moon. And of course, you can always opt for room service 24 hours a day.

Write now: Hayman Travel Offices, Sydney: 3 Knox Street, Double Bay, N.S.W. 2028, Australia. Tel: (02) 327–2255. Double rooms run from about $190 US to $340 US; suites, $470 to $540. Children from 2–15 years, pay Australian $30 per night. Maximum of two adults and one child per double room.

Time Out on Fiji

Toberua Island, Fiji

Jessica and Alan, a photographer/writer team from Los Angeles, chose Fiji for their vacation. "We went there on our honeymoon and will never forget watching one deliriously happy little family of platinum blondes from Sweden. We remarked then that it was an ideal place to go with children. Our friends thought we were crazy travelling all the way to the South Pacific with a three-month-old and a four-year-old. But actually, it was a breeze. The flight leaves at night, so we put them in their jammies and read a bedtime story. They were out in minutes." Jessica added, "We also packed a backpack for Mark and stuffed our carry-ons with toys, coloring books, pencils and little stickers. During the stopover in Honolulu, Lisa slept and Mark looked around at all the different people. Mark loved the fact that we went from a huge plane to a smaller plane, then a smaller, and finally a speedboat." Alan chimed in, "Jess and I were terrified on the small plane, but Mark had his nose pressed against the window half the time looking down at the farms and villages. The rest of the time he was asking a million questions about the pilot and all the dashboard instruments."

Guests at Toberua Island (pronounce it tom-berua if you want to sound like a Fijian) stay in individual bures (boo-rays), little thatched roof houses with woven walls that taper up to twenty-five feet. Each one has plenty of room for mom and dad and up to three kids, plus a refrigerator and tea and coffee making facilities. All fourteen of them are smack dab on a flawless beach with sliding glass doors inches away from the water's edge. There's always the sweet fruity scent of frangiapani filling the air and long-trunked palms swooshing their broomy branches high above. And everywhere you look, you see hibiscus blossoms. Fijians love flowers.

Days are devoted to taking it easy, whether it be bobbing around a silky lagoon in masks and fins, or plopping down with Trader Vic's-like drinks and enormous straw hats on your own little patch of sand. Full-time nannies are available to keep children happily occupied with shell collecting, flower stringing, and all sorts of excursions and water sports. According to Jessica, "The kids loved their Fijian lady." For grownups and children, there's a glass-bottomed boat that slides over forests of coral teeming with fluorescent fish and bubbles that look like mercury. You can also go on fishing excursions, visit postcard-perfect Fijian villages, boat over to Suva for a shopping spree, and even plant yourselves on a little cay with a picnic lunch lovingly prepared by Toberua cooks. ("We put sunscreen and a hat on Lisa and she sat in the sand totally content.") If you're up for a real adventure, consider chartering "Adi Toberua," the hotel's private yacht which comes with a captain/cook.

Evenings start off with popsicle-colored drinks and melting sunsets and then move on to dinners you'll be talking about long after you've returned home. The hotel encourages children to eat earlier than parents and afterwards return to nannies. That way, moms and dads can have long, leisurely meals. Best always is the fish—often minutes out of the water. You can have it served with a blend of fiery hot Indian spices or simply grilled with a squeeze of fresh lemon. With every meal, there are all sorts of unrecognizable local fruits and vegetables and a satiating selection of Australian, New Zealand, and California wines. The most popular finale: home-made coconut ice cream.

Write now: Toberua Island, P.O. Box 567, Suva, Fiji Islands. Tel: 26 356 (in Suva) and 49 177 (on the island). A family of four (with one child under two) staying in a bure with all meals, daily babysitting, and tax runs about $343 per day plus $37 per person airport transfers (kids under three free).

At Ease in the French West Indies

L'Habitation, Anse Marcel, St. Martin

Pat and Michael, two attorneys, wanted to thaw out. It had been a long winter in upstate New York, and they longed for some sun and heat. They had no interest in the big, glitzy, Caribbean resorts-cum-casinos, but didn't necessarily want to stay in a tiny full-of-character hotel with nothing to do. "Quite frankly," Pat told us, "we wanted to go someplace where we could be waited on hand and foot. Someplace with terrific food. And someplace where the munchkins could be taken care of while we hid behind sunglasses by a pool." Just last summer, she had torn out some pages from a magazine that had used L'Habitation (by the way, the French say "la-bee-tah-see-OWN") as a backdrop for their fashion shoot. "I remember searching maniacally for the location credit. Just seeing the architecture of this hotel made me want to go."

In March last year, they were on their way, leaving H. B. (short for Hound of the Baskevilles) with Grandma and Grandpa. "You should have seen us once the cab dropped us at the hotel," recollected Pat. "We were all decked out in crisp white tropical outfits with matching luggage. We walked into this drop-dead gorgeous lobby with high ceilings, gargantuan plants, extravagant floral arrangements, and marble everywhere thinking we looked like a Ralph Lauren ad. It wasn't until a sweet little French man politely tapped Michael on the shoulder and whispered, "excusez moi, monsieur." We looked back and saw a trail of stuffing that had been dripping out of Timmy's now-empty gorilla." That was the first of many incidents Pat and Michael turned red over. But according to Pat, "The staff seemed to get such a kick out of us. They're very used to families."

Getting settled into their suite turned out to be even funnier. "My kids are like cats," Pat explained, "whenever we go anywhere, they have to check out every single corner. We weren't there more than two minutes and five-year-old Maria came giggling out of the bathroom saying it was a square toilet. Sure enough, it was a rectangular seat." At L'Habitation, there are all sorts of progressive touches imported from France—even the coat hangers look like something that should be in the Museum of Modern Art. In the suites, there are lots of family-friendly amenities like fully-equipped kitchens and pull-out sofas. Double rooms and junior suits have kitchenettes. All accommodations are handsomely decorated in a Creole style (definition: light pastel colors, airy, by-the-sea softness) and look out at the marina or gardens.

There are numerous ways to work off the creme brulé and mousses you'll undoubtably be hooked on during your stay, including snorkeling, pedalboating, canoeing, sailing, and water skiing. The calm waters right off the beach are perfect for youngsters, but L'Habitation's pool is an even bigger hit. It has a wading pool adjoining the adults' pool and a large sitting area, so you can keep an eye on them as you slap on lotion. Drier diversions for older children include volleyball, shuffleboard, and miniature golf and croquet. And for the whole family, there's an extensive array of sports facilities at Le Privilege, a health and exercise center, up the hill from the resort and a jogging trail that wraps around the landscape. When you feel like getting away from the sea and sand, try indulging yourselves in another favorite St. Martin pastime: shopping. The surprisingly chic town of Marigot is filled with gleaming boutiques showing off their latest Parisian imports.

Gourmands go ga ga over food on St. Martin. And though

there are two great restaurants right at L'Habitation (with special children's menus), you'll want to dine elsewhere at least once or twice. For unfailingly good French cuisine, head for the one-street village of Grand Case where there may be more French restaurants than there are in the whole state of Maine.

Write now: Mondotels, Inc., 200 West 57th Street, New York, NY 10019. Tel: (212) 757–0225. Outside New York State, (800) 847–4249. The "Family Escape" package for two adults and two children runs about $1186 for seven nights. Most guestrooms have two queen-size beds and lodge kids under 12 free year round. LePrivilege facilities are complimentary to L'Habitation guests.

A Family that Skis Together . . .

Badrutt's Palace Hotel, St. Moritz, Switzerland

John and Diana met at a ski lodge in Colorado and have been spending their vacations skiing ever since. According to John, "Most ski resorts are great for children, so we're not hindered at all with our two six-year-old twin daughters." The Chicago-based couple (she's an editor, he's an investment banker) have been working their way down a list of ski destinations and decided not to wait any longer to see the jet-set favorite, St. Moritz. "We thought it would be especially fun for the girls since the Palace looks like a fairy castle," Diana explained. Indeed, Badrutt's does look a fantasy with its great tower, ornate balconies, and *fin de siècle* architecture.

The Illinois family stayed in an enormous two-bedroom suite (all rooms at the Palace can open up into the next, depending on how big your family is) with a jaw-dropping view of the mountains. Each room has refrigerators and wall-to-wall carpeting.

"This was our second season with the girls on skis," explained Diana. "Last year, they had a great instructor in Vail and were going down the green trails after two days." The first morning out, they bundled the girls up ("They looked like miniature Michelin men with their puffy ski outfits and bug-eye goggles") and joined the other beginners in the children's ski school. "We hung around a few minutes to watch and were amazed at how quickly they remembered how to do the wedge and the snowplow. We knew they were in good hands so we headed for the lifts to get in our first run of the trip. Later, the four of us met and spent the afternoon in the pool and spa."

As well as a world of winter sports on the doorstep, the indoor possibilities at Badrutt's are endless. There's an indoor swimming pool, tennis courts, squash courts, indoor golf, an ice rink, and a fitness and aerobics center. The children can take all sorts of lessons including swimming and diving, skating, and tennis. And there's a kindergarten and teacher for the little ones.

The apres-ski scene in St. Moritz always has a sparkly air of carnival that will mesmerize both you and your children. Badrutt's Grand Hall fills with flawlessly tanned, well-heeled skiers sporting boasty mink hats and one-of-a-kind sweaters that are usually found in the Neiman Marcus' of the world. You hear Swedish, Greek, French, and all sorts of unrecognizable accents in every corner of the room. There's the customary swapping of close-call trail stories and the congratulatory toasts with Cafi-Fertig, the local version of Irish Coffee.

Afterwards, there's exceptional dining right at the hotel

including French cuisine in The Restaurant and Grill and in Chesa Veglia, an old Engadine-style restaurant in a 17th century farmhouse (owned by the hotel). You can also eat very informally at the Trattoria or have dinner delivered to your suite on those zonked-out-from-the-slopes nights. The hotel has a very well-organized babysitting service so you can go from dinner to dancing without a worry.

Write now: Badrutt's Palace Hotel, St. Moritz, Switzer land. Tel: (082) 37739. Or call (800) 223-6800. In New York State, (212) 838–3110. Double rooms run from about $290 to $410 depending on the season; one bedroom suites run from about $1090 to $1500. Add another $80 for one child over five. Children under five are free. Prices include breakfasts, plus one main meal daily, taxes and service. Keep in mind that St. Moritz is also a delightful summer destination. However, it is closed April through June and early September to mid-December. February is high season.

English Elegance

Welcombe Hotel & Golf Course, Stratford-upon-Avon

Jean, a New York-based pianist, wife and mother, was thrilled. Her agent had booked her a concert at Wigmore Hall in London. "After talking it over, my husband Evan and I decided to make it a business-cum-family vacation trip." They figured they'd spend a few days in London and then rent a car and head out to the countryside.

Jean said they chose the Welcombe Hotel & Golf Course because they wanted to live like royalty for a week right in the heart of the English countryside. They had looked into several English Country manor house hotels but got the impression that children were merely tolerated, not necessarily encouraged. "We heard the Welcombe had nannies and that there was lots for kids to do. And since it's in Shakespeare country, we thought it would be a fun way to introduce our twelve-year-old son Daniel to English literature. Evan thought this would be a good idea considering he's a novelist himself."

The hotel, an exceedingly beautiful Jacobean-style mansion built in 1869, is surrounded by immaculately maintained green lawns and formal gardens. It was originally built to have one window for each day of the year, and there are quite a few chimneys as well.

On the grounds, you'll find eighteen holes of golf, (and a putting green with child-size golf putters), table tennis, and some traditional Cotswold games (dice). Horseback riding, squash, croquet, fishing, and tennis can be arranged.

Though the rooms in the newer Garden Wing are very attractive, try to get one of the old manor house rooms for the full Olde English affect. They're handsomely decorated with antiques and period paintings, and Country English fabrics, some have four-poster canopy beds and fireplaces. All rooms have wall to wall carpeting and mini bars. There's also 24-hour room service.

Mornings at the Welcombe start with hot breakfast delivered with the paper to your room. In addition to the traditional teas, coffees, juices, and toasts, you can order porridges, grilled kippers, or haddock. If you need anything specially prepared for the children, the staff is bend-over backwards accommodating. Afterwards, you can follow the well-trod footpaths that lead into town (about a mile and a half) to visit the birthplace and former residences of

Shakespeare and other Tudor houses each boasting some Shakespearean claim to fame. You may also want to take the children on a steamer excursion down the River Avon. Or follow the path to Shottery (one mile west) where you'll find Anne Hathway's Cottage, a beautifully preserved thatched farmhouse children usually are delightfully intrigued by. You can watch local craftspeople demonstrate their works. Nearby, order a creamy quiche or ploughman's lunch (salads and cheeses) at Truffles Olde Tea Shoppe, along with some richly-brewed Earl Grey.

By car, you can easily reach the Cotwolds, one of Britain's most intensely scenic chunks of countryside stretching over some 600-odd miles. The wolds are made up of puffy little hills holding shiny black lakes as if precious jewels. You'll pass through one tidy village after another, each centerpieced by a church with a steeple that seems to scrape the sky. You'll see riders in full English habit and country gentlemen walking their King Charles spaniels. You'll discover all sorts of marvelous little shops selling horsey prints and place mats, chintz-covered pillows and Country English patterned bags (great for baby paraphernalia), British teas and soaps, and one gleaming antique shop after another. You can also find some great wool shops selling sweaters, socks, and scarves, equestrian shops, and leather goods (the dowdy looking pocketbooks the Queen carries are coming back). Stow-on-the-Wold is a must if you have girls. There's a doll shop/hospital where you can buy eyeballs, arms, legs, or whatever else might be missing.

Tea time by the Welcombe's fireplace is worth rushing back for, but do try some of the cozy tea shops tucked away in every Cotswoldian village. Over a pot of brewing Earl Grey, and a platter of scones with clotted cream and jams, you can plan your next day's exploring routes. By the way, if you've ever thought tea time was a leisure activity reserved for the grandma and grandpas of the world, you—and especially your children—will be delighted to find the tea rooms bustling with young British families.

Every night, the Welcombe's formal restaurant fills with guest and local Brits, and serves skillfully prepared food, including French specialties, such as breast of duck with a black currant and liqueur sauce.

Do order tickets for a play at the Royal Shakespeare Theatre well in advance (the season runs from April through January). The hotel will gladly arrange theater tickets in advance upon receipt of payment.

Write now: The Welcombe Hotel & Golf Course, Warvick Road, Stratford-upon-Avon, CV37 ONR, England. Tel: 0789 295252. In New York, call (212) 839-0222. Nationwide (800) 237-1236. One-bedroom suites run about $140 to $250 per night inclusive of full English breakfast, service and V.A.T. Adjoining double rooms are available at $105 per night (also includes breakfast, service and V.A.T.) no extra charge for children under two. Fifty percent reduction for children under twelve.

Magic Number

If you need some hand-holding in your planning, contact Rascals in Paradise, a full-service travel agency that specializes in family travel. They'll take care of all the details whether they be getting bumper pads on cribs or arranging for distilled water for breast-feeding moms. They have an extensive list of tried-and-true hotels around the world and will see to it that your trip is flawless.

Example #2: A roundup of honeymoon ideas for Bridal Guide

SHORT BUT SWEET HONEYMOONS
by Susan Farewell

You finally got the wedding plans firmed up. The church. The reception hall. Coordinating family schedules. Only one problem: it's the height of the season at your office and skipping town for a week or so isn't exactly going to keep you on the corporate ladder.

Relax. You're in the 90s. Honeymoons no longer have to be by the book. You have options.

One option is to take a short honeymoon right after the wedding and plan to get away for a couple weeks when the two of you have more time. Another option is to take a short honeymoon, period. Why not? Why not spend four intensely wonderful days together doing all the things you love to do every minute of the time.

From a financial point of view, it certainly makes sense. Instead of spreading the honeymoon budget thin over a week or two, you can do it up in style and make absolutely every moment count.

On the following pages, you'll find a potpourri of wedding-trip possibilities, all of which lend themselves beautifully to four day visits. And though each one offers a very different brand of romance, they all just hit the spot for couples like you who want to make their short honeymoon sweeter than ever.

Horsing Around at a Dude Ranch

You're probably just reading this out of curiosity. "Who, in their right mind," you think, "would go to a dusty old horse farm on their honeymoon?" Well, dear reader, *you* might.

Whether you don't know the difference between English and Western or you've always fantasized about living on a ranch, you'll find American dude ranches are not only a lot of fun, but remarkably romantic. Oh, and by the way, they're not all dusty old farms. Throughout the American West, there are dude ranches that look like they'd be right at home on the pages of *House and Garden* magazine.

In many of these, guests stay in private log cabins that are not only attractively furnished (with western artwork and Indian blankets throughout), but are deliriously comfortable with big sink-into couches, thick rugs, and working fireplaces. Most have jaw-droppingly beautiful views (when a place has Yellowstone or the Rocky Mountains for its backyard, what do you expect?), and private terraces or patios out of which you can stare for hours. A handful of ranches even have lovely little touches like fresh wild flowers in the room and turn-down service at night.

At all dude ranches, there's a combination platter of activities to take your pick of. In the daytime, you can saddle up and join a trail ride into the mountains (by the way, beginners are welcome), watch a crowd-roaring rodeo, cast a line in a river that shines like mica, hit tennis balls on a court you don't have to wait in line for, or use the time to totally relax. Many ranches have pools complete with floats for bobbing around while you gaze at the clouds. Some have hot tubs set into the landscape like precious gems.

In the evenings, a bell usually announces dinner, and ranch guests—glowing from all the fresh air and outdoor adventures—meet in the main dining room for big family-style meals. The food is generally hearty ranch fare: heaping platters of ribs, piles of corn on the cob, good old American mashed potatoes, stir-fried vegetables. Almost always, breads and desserts are baked on the premises from recipes that have been passed down through the generations. One night, there may be a chuck wagon dinner up in the mountains or a steak cookout under a sky full of stars. Later on, there's usually something else to look forward to like a square dance, a yodeling contest, or a bonfire around which wranglers tell stories while eager listeners toast marshmallows.

Though you'll find dozens of dude ranches to take your pick of, here are four that are especially honeymoon-friendly.

In Tucson, Arizona, the White Stallion Ranch (602-297-0252) hosts its guest in spotless adobe cabins on 3000 acres at the foot of the Tucson Mountains.

Wind River Ranch (303-583-4212) in Estes Park, Colorado is surrounded by magnificent Rocky Mountain scenery.

The fittingly-named Paradise Guest Ranch (307-684-7876) in Buffalo, Wyoming has impeccably appointed cabins with can't-take-your-eyes-off-it views of the Bighorn Mountains looming all around.

Lone Mountain Ranch (406-995-4644) in Big Sky, Montana is one of the most progressive-minded dude ranches around with a long list of non-equestrian activities, including bird walks, fly-fishing lessons, orienteering workshops, and nature hikes to nearby Yellowstone National Park.

For a dude ranch nearest you, contact The Dude Rancher's Association (303-493-7623). For information on Colorado dude ranches, call: Colorado Dude & Guest Ranch Association (800-441-6060, or 303-887-3128).

So dude, perhaps it's time to shine up the cowboy boots, make sure the old jeans fit, shop for a pair of bandannas and start thinking about your honeymoon home on the range.

Mellowing Out at a Country Lodge

"We just want to go someplace and crash for a couple of days." Sound like you? You're not alone. After months of picking out flowers, invitations, the church music, the menu, the band—the last thing many couples want to do is go sightseeing or live out of suitcases for two weeks.

Why not stay in a grand old country lodge? Some wonderfully warm place where you can stay put and just relax together. Unlike full-fledged resorts where you may spend your days switching from bathing suits to tennis whites to golf clothes, lodges are more conducive to just taking it easy for awhile. And though most offer a handful of active diversions, there's no pressure to have to do anything. Country lodges are usually bigger than inns and have their own dining rooms, which means you never have to leave for meals. They often don't have telephones and TVs in individual guest rooms.

There are several country lodges in the United States, some in elegantly appointed historic buildings that have been welcoming honeymooners for years. Traditionally, they're centerpieced by big lounge areas complete with stone fireplaces around which guests relax in the kinds of couches and chairs you never want to get out of. You can spend hours sipping tea or brandy as you gaze into the fire together, mingle with fellow guests, or finally plunge into the huge hardcovers you never had a chance to read at home. It's probably the first time in months you've had a chance to just "be" with each other. No decisions to make. No calls to be returned. Just the two of you and a chunk of unstructured time in a beautiful place.

Most lodges are cradled in spectacularly scenic landscapes which offer fresh-aired diversions when you feel slightly ambitious. You might take out a rowboat and sing as you paddle off into oblivion or follow trails on foot or horseback. Some also have swimming pools, a tennis court or two, and a couple of spa facilities (sauna, steam, whirlpool tubs) as well as game rooms where you can challenge each other to a game of ping-pong or pool.

Eating well is one of the real pleasures of staying at a lodge (most of which have equally good reputations for their food). You can start off the day by having breakfast in your bathrobes on your terrace and end the day with a table d'hote dinner elegantly served in a dining room amid flickering candles, fine china and glassware, and shining silver.

Your travel agent can help you find a country retreat close to home. In the meantime, here are four that get our honeymoon seal of approval.

El Tovar Hotel (602-638-2401) is perched on the south rim of the Grand Canyon in Arizona. A grand old established hotel, it was built in 1908 of native boulders and Oregon pine. There are plenty of hiking trails to follow.

Jenny Lake Lodge (307-543-2855) is magnificently situated in the Grand Tetons in Wyoming. Guests stay in log cabins which are comfortably furnished with hand-made quilts and braided rugs. Activities include hiking, biking, and trail riding.

Lake Quinault Lodge (206-288-2571) is poised on the shores of glacier-fed Lake Quinault on the Olympic Peninsula in Washington. Its wood-beamed and massive stone fireplaced central lounge and long lake-viewing veranda are always abuzz with healthy looking guests who come to enjoy the scenic splendors of the lake, the Olympic Mountains, and surrounding rain forests.

Trapp Family Lodge (802-253-8511) in Stowe, Vermont prides itself on its Austrian ambience. In winter, it's a magnet for cross-country skiers who come from all over to glide along its trails that look like a snowy paper weight come alive. The other seasons bring on hikers, leaf lookers, and fresh-air seekers.

Going Goofy in Theme Parks

Go ahead. Put on the Mickey Mouse ears and throw your sophisticated image to the wind. Theme parks are not only dreams come true for the short-set, but can be wildly romantic for honeymooners.

Just think of the possibilities: the dark spook houses where you get really, really scared and cling to each other for security. The gaily painted carousel transporting you both back to your make-believe childhoods. The miniature car race where you can roar alongside each other, foot peddles glued to the floor.

Your honeymoon is a perfect time to go to an amusement park. It gives you a chance to "decompress" after months of planning the wedding. Your biggest decision of the day may be whether to take the simulated shuttle to Mars or to ride the Space Mountain roller coaster for the umpteenth time. Three or four days is just enough time to stuff yourselves on fun. Some theme parks even offer special discounted "passports" which cover admission and unlimited rides and attractions for that amount of time.

Walt Disney World in Florida is where you'll find the biggest selection of amusement park activities. On its 27,400 acres, there are three separate constellations of entertainment including the fantastic Magic Kingdom, the eye-poppingly progressive Epcot Center, and the new MGM Studios Theme Park where you can tour animation production facilities, sound stages, and street sets where Disney and Touchstone films are shot.

You can actually stay right at Disney World in one of its "on campus" hotels, resorts, or villa complexes, or even pitch a tent on its campground. That way, you don't have to deal with commuting to the "World" (all Disney accommodations have access to the bus, boat, and monorail transportation systems), plus you get preferential treatment in making dinner-show reservations and some admission discounts. There's also a special magic to staying in this wonderful world of fantasy. The most luxurious accommodations include the Contemporary Resort Hotel, the Polynesian Village Resort, and the new Grand Floridian Beach Resort. All three are big lake-front hotels connected to the Magic Kingdom and Epcot Center by monorail. The Floridian Beach Resort has special "honeymoon rooms" in red-roofed turrets (the hotel is modeled after a 19th-century Floridian resort); some look out at the Magic Kingdom. For information on all the Walt Disney World accommodations, call (407) 824-4321 or write: Walt Disney World Information, P.O. Box 10040, Lake Buena Vista, FL 32830-0040.

Though not quite as extensive as the Florida property, Disneyland is a mecca for amusement park aficionados. The highlight of its 76 acres is a ride called "Star Tour" in which visitors are ushered aboard StarSpeeders which blast off on a madcap flight to the Moon of Endor, using the same flight simulator technology used to train military and commercial pilots.

Though there are no hotels at Disneyland itself, there are several within two or three miles of the park, many with special features and park admissions included in room rates. The most conveniently located hotel is the Disneyland Hotel (714-778-6600) which has direct monorail service to the Magic Kingdom. You could actually spend a good chunk of your honeymoon here alone. You can swim, play tennis, feed koi fish, watch a light show, shop, dine, drink, dance—you name it! There are also two Hyatts nearby, the Hyatt Alicante (714-971-3000) and the Hyatt Anaheim (714-772-5900). Both are high-tech, bustling properties with a selection of restaurants, shops, and other amenities. For a complete listing of nearby hotels, write: Anaheim Area Visitor and Convention Bureau, P.O. Box 4270, Anaheim, CA 92803 or call: (714) 999-8999.

If you don't happen to live near these theme parks, you'll find plenty in between including Dollywood in Pigeon Forge, Tennessee (for Dolly Parton fans), Hersheypark in Hershey, Pennsylvania (a Hershey Bar and a Reese's Cup are two of the chocolate-flavored characters that stroll the park's grounds), Opryland in Nashville, Tennessee (where musicians from around the world come to perform), and Cedar Point in Sandusky, Ohio (which has more roller coasters—a total of 7—than any other U.S. park). Almost every state has a theme park of some sort. For a list of them, contact the International Association of Amusement Parks and Attractions, 4230 King Street, Alexandria, VA 22302; (703) 671-5800.

"Going to Town" in a Big City

Have you ever really "done the town?" Sure you've gone out on the town for dinner and a show. Everyone has. But how about doing it up like you've never done before on your honeymoon. Stay in an outrageously luxurious hotel or inn, take in a handful of museums, shop (or window-shop) up a storm, eat at restaurants you've read about, and get tickets to a big-name show or a major-league game. For your honeymoon, choose a city that's a natural romantic. Where just being there is a thrill.

New Orleans is such a place. Its legendary French Quarter is filled with European-flavored romance, world-renowned jazz, and spicy Creole cuisine.

You can spend long leisurely hours strolling the narrow-cobbled streets or better yet, take it all in from a clip-clopping horse-drawn carriage. You can sample New Orleans' gumbo, po'boy sandwiches, and red beans and rice. Sip *cafe au lait* and sample *beignets* in the French Market. At night, move on to Bourbon Street, one big open-air party that happens year-round, 24 hours a day. The French Quarter is home to dozens of unbelievably charming inns such as Soniat House (504-522-0570), a perfect Southern inn with high-ceilinged rooms, four-poster beds, Victorian love seats, and other antique furnishings and Hotel Maison de Ville (504-561-5858) where guests can stay in private cottages replete with antique furnishings, etched glass, and Oriental carpets. Outside the quarter, you'll find the Fairmont Hotel (504-529-7111), New Orleans' *grande dame* of hotels.

For more information, contact the Greater New Orleans Tourist & Convention Commission, (504) 566-5011.

San Francisco is another city where you're sure to find

romance in the air. A series of hills crested with gingerbread mansions and glass-and-chrome towers, it's one of the world's most captivating cities, especially when the fog horns blow, the sea gulls soar overhead, and the cable cars trundle by.

You can take your time exploring its patchwork of neighborhoods taking breaks in the dozens of bohemian coffee shops. Be sure to walk up to Telegraph Hill from which you can see the bay either bundled in fog or clear as a window with the Golden Gate Bridge hogging your attention. Window-shop on Union Square. Watch the sea lions that have colonized the docks off Fisherman's Wharf. Eat dim sum in Chinatown or Italian in North Beach. The list goes on and on. The city's most celebrated hotels include the Fairmont (415-772-5000) with unmatched views, the Stanford Court (415-989-3500) a Nob Hill classic, and the Four Seasons Clift Hotel (415-775-4700) a world-class hotel on Union Square.

For more information, contact the San Francisco Convention & Visitors Bureau, (415) 974-6900.

Manhattan-style romance takes form in many ways. The citiest city there is, it's *the* place to dress to the nines, shop 'til you drop, dine and dance like you've never dined and danced before. Your best bet is to approach it as if it were a box of chocolates—sampling a bit of everything and not dwelling on anything you both don't like. By day, maybe poke around the Upper East Side museums, browse in the famous midtown stores like Tiffany's and Saks, and take your pick of sightseeing options (the Empire State Building, the Statue of Liberty, Ellis Island—just to name a few). Be sure to take time out to relax though. Perhaps spend an afternoon having British tea at the Salon in the Stanhope Hotel or Little Nell's Tea Room. Or wander through Central Park, stopping to watch the roller-skater's disco, the volleyball game du jour, the character that plays great jazz on a piano he wheels around with him. At night, splurge at a high-perched restaurant like the Rainbow Room or Windows on the World. For staying, pick someplace wonderful right in the core of the Apple like The Plaza (212-759-3000), the Ritz-Carlton Hotel (212-757-1900), or the St. Moritz on-the-Park (212-755-5800)—all with magnificent views of Central Park and the city lights.

For more information, contact the New York Convention and Visitors Bureau, (212) 397-8200.

As you can see, taking a short honeymoon is not a compromise at all. After spending four outrageously wonderful days together at a place you both love, you'll feel totally invigorated and have just as many memories as the couple who spends two weeks in the Caribbean or Europe. And remember, you're a 90s couple—anything goes.

Sometimes, travel pieces are combined with sport stories, profiles, or other topics. The following is a profile piece, but involves travel and a sporting event.

Example #1: For Golf Illustrated *magazine*

GOING TO EXTREMES
by Susan Farewell

"It's out! Hurry, the sun is out!" shouted club pro David Barnwell as if he were Paul Revere announcing the coming of the British troops. It was exactly five minutes before midnight at the fifth annual Arctic Open at the Akureyri Golf Club in northern Iceland.

The handful of photographers who had traveled up to the world's northernmost 18-hole golf course (only fifty miles from the Arctic Circle) to photograph the all-night tournament put down their hot chocolates, zipped up their parkas, and rushed out of the clubhouse, tripods and cameras dangling from their shoulders. The mission: to get at least one photograph proving that the sun really does shine through the night. The facts: it had been drizzling since tee time, the temperature had dropped to the mid-40s, and the sun . . . what sun?

Barnwell was clearly relieved when old Helios decided to make a midnight appearance, but not at all surprised. A transplanted Englishman, he has acclimated himself very well to the predictable unpredictableness of the local weather. He has also adapted very well to the very short—a mere three months—golf season in northern Iceland.

Barnwell, who is thirty years old, came to Akureyri from Harrogate, England, where he was the assistant pro at the Moor Allerton Golf Club in Leeds, under pro Peter Blaze. His primary reason for leaving England was the opportunity to become a club pro. He saw a lot of promise in Akureyri in that golf can be played through the night. Indeed, though the season is short, one can play from sunup to sundown, in other words, 24 hours a day, since the sun hardly dips below the horizon in midsummer.

Barnwell also recognized that there is great interest in the sport in Iceland. In fact, about one in every fifteen residents of Akureyri is a member of the club. "Icelanders play a lot of sports, many different sports. For example, children will play golf, badminton, football, and then, of course, ski," he explained. "And all ages are athletic in Iceland. Right now, I am teaching a 75-year-old man who just took up the sport."

Barnwell, by his own admission, has also adapted well to

the local customs. On a typical weekend night in Akureyri, people from all over Iceland (including many from Reykjavik—a five-hour-drive away) go to the discos in Akureyri. When they close at 3 A.M., everyone congregates in the town center, and socializes until 6 or 7 A.M. "From there, sometimes I have to go right into work at half past eight."

When asked if he was a night owl in England, he replied emphatically, "Not at all!" It just goes to show, that when in Iceland, one must do as the Icelanders.

14.2 Travel Advertorials

Basically, an advertorial is a sales tool a magazine or newspaper uses to bring in ads. It's those pages or sections you see that sometimes look—and often sound, editorial—but have the word ADVERTISEMENT clearly written on each page.

Ideas for advertorials almost always originate at the publication itself. They are often overseen and assigned by the promotion director or someone in the advertising department. These assignments generally pay well and are usually assigned to established writers who specialize in certain geographical areas or types of travel.

The biggest difference between an advertorial and an editorial is that an advertorial must be positive about a place while an editorial could be negative. In other words, in an editorial piece you might tell a reader to avoid a certain beach because it's polluted. In an advertorial, the writer simply would not mention the beach. However, as you can see by the following sample advertorials and the editorials earlier in this book, there are not necessarily any differences in content. In fact, the object is to write an advertorial so it sounds like an editorial.

Example #1: For Metropolitan Home *magazine*

ONTARIO OUTRAGEOUS
by Susan Farewell

Time Out in Toronto

Toronto is a patchwork of neighborhoods where the food, the arts, the fashion, and the shops are all very exciting.

Culture Vultures will be happy to know that there's no end to the performing arts scene in Toronto. Along with the National Ballet Company, The Canadian Opera, and the Toronto Symphony, there are hundreds of other stage performances every night of the week from small repertory groups to London shows.

The Museum Scene is as impressive with the recently renovated Royal Ontario Museum (the ROM) topping the list with its mind-boggling collection of Chinese antiquities. Two other museums to pencil in on your vacation calendar are the George R. Gardiner Museum (stunning ceramics) and the Art Gallery of Ontario which houses the world's largest collection of Henry Moore pieces.

What's In Store for shoppers? Originals you'll not find elsewhere. Look for Quebec folk art, Eskimo carvings, early Canadian country furniture and baskets intricately woven by Indians. Make your way to The Algonquians (670 Queen Street West), a trove of authentic Indian arts and crafts and The Guild Shop (140 Cumberland Street), a showcase of pottery, jewelry, woodcarvings, textiles, glass, and leather creations by over one hundred Canadian artisans. For antiques, don't miss Sunday mornings at the Harbourfront Antique Market (222 Queen's Quay West), when hundreds of dealers converge to show their wares. And be sure to take a jaunt through Eaton Center (enter on Yonge Street), an enormous shopping mall based on the Galleria in Milan.

Elsewhere in Toronto, you'll find all sorts of boutiques that reflect the city's souffle of inhabitants. Some neighborhoods to scout out are Yorkville (rife with chic designer shops and sun-splashed outdoor cafes); St. Clair West (Toronto's Little Italy); Chinatown (complete with hold-your-nose fish markets and fabric stores piled high with imported silks); Queen Street West (a magnet for New Wave Canadian designers) and Kensington Market, even if you're not "in the market" for fruits and vegetables or Portuguese pots and pans.

Torontonians dine out a lot and it's easy to understand why. The city's home to a satiating selection of restaurants, many chef-owned. Some names to know are Fenton's, 2 Gloucester St. (961-8485) with an ever-changing Continental menu and a lengthy wine list; Bremelmans, 83 Bloor Street West (960-0306) and Bellair Cafe, 100–104 Cumberland (964-2222) for nouvelle cuisine and Metropolis, 838 Yonge Street (924-4100) known for its Canadian fare. Auberge Gavroche, 90 Avenue Road (920-0956), Maison Basque, 15 Temperance Street (368-6146), and Les Copains, 48 Wellington Street East (869-0898) are three unfailingly good French finds. Cafe Victoria in the King Edward Hotel at 37 King Street (863-9700) is best for Sunday brunch or tea. The Old Fish Market, 12 Market Street (363-0334), is a casual seafood place with a loyal local clientele and Pink Pearl, 142 Dundas Street (977-3388), is admired for its dim sum. For more information on Toronto, write now: Metropolitan Toronto Convention & Visitors Association, P.O. Box 126, Toronto, Canada M5J 1A7, or call: (416) 368-9990.

Capitalize on Ottawa

Canada's *petite* capital has been making the news quite a bit these days. Last year two national landmarks opened: The National Gallery of Canada (a stop-in-your-tracks-and-stare glass building designed by architect Moshe Safdie) and the avant-garde, delta-shaped National Aviation Museum. On June 29 this year, the futuristic looking Canadian Museum of Civilization will open on the banks of the Ottawa River. This of course calls for a party and Ottawa sure is good at throwing parties. In fact, no matter what time of year you visit, you'll find an event going on whether it's the Hot Air Balloon Festival or the Ottawa Winter Fair.

During summer months visitors are treated to the Changing the Guard ceremony on the billiard green lawns of Parliament Hill. There are also walking tours around the grounds, dramatic sound and light shows, and hauntingly beautiful carillon concerts.

Festivities and pomp aside, Ottawa is quite simply, a likeable city. You can do all your exploring *a pied* or rent a bike (during fair-weather months of course) to follow the paths alongside the Rideau Canal. You can also take a nautical sightseeing trip on one of the boats that glides up and down the canal.

Now for some Shop Talk. The Sparks Street Mall, a five-block-long mall, is one of the biggest shopping areas of Ottawa. Some of its most interesting shops include Four Corners (93 Sparks Street) and Davis Agency Canadiana Shop (203 Sparks Street) which carry Canadian crafts. Another worthwhile stop is Snow Goose (83 Sparks Street) with a gallery of native Canadian art. The Rideau Centre, a *tres moderne* shopping mall downtown has over two hundred boutiques to browse through.

For culinary explorations, start with tea at Zoe's in the Chateau Laurier, 1 Rideau (232-6411), one of Canada's most elegant hotels. Save The Courtyard Restaurant, 21 George Street (238-4623) for Sunday brunch when there's live classical music. The Ritz on The Canal, 375 Queen Elizabeth's Driveway (238-8998) is a delightful spot to stop for lunch while biking (they're famous for their little pizzas). Around the market area, you'll find a multitude of restaurants serving everything from vegetarian to Moroccan. Extra special is Le Jardin, 127 York Street (238-1828) for French cuisine. For the biggest selection of French restaurants though, cross over to Hull, a French-speaking city linked to Ottawa by several bridges (both Ottawa and Hull make up Canada's National Capital Region).

Apres Dark hours in Ottawa are spent sipping libations in wine bars in Lower Town or attending performances at the National Arts Centre (65 Elgin Street). For More Information on Ottawa, write now: Canada's Capital Vistors and Convention Bureau, 222 Queen Street, 7th floor, Ottawa, Canada K1P 5V9, or call: (613) 237-5150.

Example #2: For Your Invitation to Europe (*a travel supplement distributed in the* New York Times)

SKIING EUROPE: THE PEAKS OF PERFECTION

by Susan Farewell

Skiing in Europe sounds like something only exceptionally privileged Americans get to do. You picture them as extraordinarily wealthy, well-traveled, beautiful, frightfully fit, and famous (or at the very least, related to some bold-faced name).

Think what you want, but the truth is the door to skiing in Europe is wide open for anyone. Of course, you'll see spandex-clad socialites effortlessly zigzagging down trails and you might just find yourself crammed up against a face you last saw on the cover of *People* magazine in a cable car. Still, skiing in Europe is not reserved for a fortunate few.

For one thing, it need not be as expensive as you imagine. Thanks to a series of highly competitive air/land ski packages, you could keep your budget under a $1000 for a week, which—all said and done—is about as much as you'd spend traveling to the Rockies from the east coast.

And getting there is not necessarily more time-consuming than getting to some of the U.S. resorts thanks to direct flights, high-speed trains, and super-efficient autobahns and road systems. Try rewinding your memory tape and tally up how many hours you spent driving up to Stowe, or flying out to Stapleton and connecting for your flight to Crested Butte. It can end up taking the same amount of time.

What about jet lag, you ask? It's inevitable whether you head east or west. Still, you couldn't find a better cure than sunshine and icy pure air. And besides, if you follow a proper diet, and slowly adjust your body clock, you need not suffer at all.

Still, is it necessary to travel *all* the way across the Atlantic to ski? Absolutely. Skiing in Europe—whether downhill or cross-country—is an experience that has no equal in the world. Nearly all of the Olympics Winter Games have taken place here. Come February, Albertville, France (by the way, don't pronounce the "t"; it's Al-bear-veal) along with eleven other Savoie resorts will become one enormous open-aired theater with 1500 athletes from around the world competing for gold and glory. This will be France's third Winter Games;

the very first games were held in Chamonix in 1924 and in 1968, they were held in Grenoble). In 1994, they'll take place in Lillehammer, Norway.

But there's more. Where else in the world can you ski from country to country? Or soar down unmarked—*off-piste*—trails? Where else could you count on finding exceptionally good food and wines on top of every mountain? Where else can you spend the morning learning how to telemark and the afternoon looking at some of the world's masterpiece paintings or shopping for eiderdown?

On the following pages, you'll find a roundup of some of the most celebrated resorts and ski areas in the Alps and Scandinavia. You'll also find sample air/hotel packages for each (prices are per person, based on double occupancy). For additional information, see your travel agent.

The Alps

These monumental mountains—which ramble through south central Europe—offer an entire galaxy of ski areas extending from southern France through Switzerland, Italy, Germany, and Austria, and into Yugoslavia and Albania. And though they share much of the same snow, the same weather, and the same mountains, like the keys of a piano, they're all a little different.

French Alps

To say the French are going all-out this year for the Winter Olympics is not an exaggeration, it's an understatement. For the event, the Savoie Region of the French Alps is being transformed into the most high-tech, efficient, *formidable* ski destination in the world. Over a billion dollars has already been invested to make these games the biggest, the most exciting, and the most memorable ever.

High-powered, masterly engineered, futuristic-looking skiing facilities are nothing new to the French, however. The country is known for its ultra-modern lifts that look like something out of a Sci-Fi movie. France also invented the concept of ski-in, ski-out resorts, which means you can step into your bindings at your hotel door, and ski off. The country is known for its mega-ski areas, which are all linked by an impressive network of lifts and runs and covered by one lift pass.

The most extensive such network is Les Trois Vallees (Courchevel, Meribel, and Val-Thorens) which will be a major hub of the Winter Games. Between these three areas, there is a combination-platter of atmospheres and skiing terrains and a grand total of 375 miles of marked runs and 200 different lifts. *Sample package:* (Courchevel): $1738 includes air, transfers, seven nights' stay, taxes, gratuities, breakfasts and dinners. Adventures on Skis, (800) 628-9655.

If you're interested in going for the Olympics (February 8 and 23), call Olson TravelWorld (800) 874-1992. At press time, there were still hotel rooms available and a handful of tickets to events, though the pickings were slim. You can ski during those weeks. Though some runs will be closed for competitions and practice, most will be open for public skiing.

Though the French take their skiing very seriously, they also believe in punctuating their days with elaborate lunchtime meals. Atop most mountains, you will find serious restaurants (not hot dog and hamburger grills), crowded with diners feasting on everything from crepes and omelettes to grilled meats and fish flown in from the Mediterranean, and—of course—celestial French wines. For Americans not in the habit of taking such long leisurely lunches, this is an ideal time to ski; lift lines are considerably shorter.

And the French know how to enjoy their time once the lifts close. After all, *apres-ski* is a French expression. Almost immediately, outdoor tables fill with spirited skiers swopping close-call trail stories. Later, following another completely satiating meal, *la vie de la nuit* is in full swing from 1 A.M.–4 A.M. in night clubs and discos.

Swiss Alps

Mention the Alps, and many Americans automatically think Switzerland. Indeed, Switzerland holds the heart of these serrated peaks, and for many *is* what skiing in Europe means.

Their international fame is well-founded. As well as being truly blessed with natural skiing assets, these Alps reap the benefits of the country's unflagging commitment to perfection. Here, you can expect nonpareil service and accommodation.

One of the most popular for North Americans is St. Moritz, the doyenne of winter resorts. This two-time Olympics Winter Games host boasts six ski areas with a total of 150 miles of groomed trails. And though skiing its runs is enough to completely exhaust even crackerjack skiers, the *apres ski* scene is especially sparkly. Every afternoon, the Grand Hall of Badrutt's Palace fills with flawlessly tanned, well-heeled skiers sporting boasty mink hats and one-of-a-kind sweaters. In all sorts of unrecognizable accents and languages, congratulatory toasts are made with Cafi-Fertig, the local version of Irish coffee. *Sample package:* $999 includes air, transfers, seven night's stay, breakfast or MAP (depending on hotel). A & S Travel Center, (800) 523-5279.

Many people go to Zermatt just because it's home to the legendary Matterhorn. No one ever regrets it. This massive landmark—which we've all seen on postcards—and its deliriously quaint (and car-free) village *is* Switzerland—exactly as you pictured it. It's situated at the end of a long valley and bounded by three ski areas—with more than 141 miles of marked trails. *Sample package:* $899 includes air, transfers, 7 night's stay, breakfast or MAP (depending on hotel). A & S Travel Center, (800) 523-5279.

Though it doesn't have the sophistication of St. Moritz or the charm of Zermatt, Davos is known for having some of the best skiing in the world. It's a ski city, rather than a ski village, surrounded by five ski areas which insure plenty of diversity and runs for every level. *Sample package:* $995 includes air, transfers, seven night's hotel stay. Alphorn Tours Inc., (215) 794–ALPS.

Italian Alps

Northern Italy is home to some of Europe's most spectacular mountains including the entire Dolomite range. It's also where some of the best ski bargains can be found and some of the best food and wines.

Perhaps the most international of all Alpine resorts is Courmayeur which lies at the junction of Switzerland, France, and Italy. Here, you can stuff yourselves on skiing Mount Blanc (Europe's highest), and if that's not enough, head for nearby Cervinia and Thuile (in Italy), Chamonix in

France, and Verbier in Switzerland. If you can force yourselves away from the slopes, you'll find the culturally-vibrant cities of Geneva, Milan, and Torina close by as well as the Val d'Aosta all around which is dotted with Italian castles. *Sample package:* $876 includes air, transfers, seven night's stay with breakfasts, hotel service charges and taxes. Central Holiday Tours, (800) 526-6045.

Italy's most famous resort is Cortina d'Ampezzo (everyone drops the "d'Ampezzo"), which hosted the 1956 Olympics. Spectacularly situated in the Dolomite Alps, it offers some of the country's most varied skiing terrain. One of the biggest advantages of skiing in the Dolomites is the "Dolomite Superski Pass" which covers almost 500 lifts and nearly 700 miles of runs in a total of thirty-five neighboring resorts. The village of Cortina is achingly beautiful with its slender-steepled Romanesque church, its pedestrians-only thoroughfare, its profusion of shops and restaurants, and the jagged Dolomite peaks all around. *Sample package:* $999 includes air, transfers, eight night's stay. A & S Travel Center, (800) 523-5279.

At all Italian ski resorts, you'll find lunch-time meals are prolonged affairs. Yes, even when the skiing conditions are flabergastingly good. And somehow, by the end of a week's stay, even the most fanatical of American skiers—who seize those liftline-less hours to ski—can be seen lingering over lobster ravioli in a cream sauce or oohing and aahing over the dessert selection. *Apres-ski* means gearing up for yet another big meal which virtually fills the evening hours.

Bavarian Alps

Most of Germany's major ski resorts are located in Bavaria, the country's southernmost state which is super-convenient for Americans because of its proximity to the Munich airport.

The country's biggest and most widely praised area is Garmisch-Partenkirchen, two towns backed by Zugspitze, Germany's highest peak. Here you'll find trails for all levels. One of the highlights of any trip—for both skiers, and non-skiers—is the cog railroad ride from Eibsee to the Zugspitzplatt, a glacier on the side of the mountain. The ride takes over an hour, passing through dense Alpine scenery. *Sample package:* $1109 includes air, seven night's stay, breakfasts, transfers, and taxes. American Express Travel Service, (800) 241-1700.

Apres-ski in the Bavaria Alps means big clunky mugs of beer or *Gluhwein* (mulled wine) in mountain lodges and later, hearty meals of sausages, sauerkraut, and all sorts of unpronounceable Bavarian delicacies.

Austrian Alps

A word you will unquestionably learn while skiing in Austria is *Gemutlichkeit*, which describes the atmosphere of most Austrian ski resorts—a wonderful synonym for the English words "cozy," "charming," and "friendly." It is a fitting description of Austrian ski resorts, most of which have chalet-style mountain lodges, horse-drawn sleighs complete with jingling bells, and hulking mountains looming all around.

However, one of the most popular destinations for North Americans—Innsbrook—is not exactly oozing with *gemutlichkeit*. After all, Innsbrook is a major European hub. Still, as capital of the Austrian Tyrol and two-time Winter Olympic Games host (in 1964 and 1976), it has five different ski areas within easy reach *plus* nearby St. Anton, Ischgl, Kitzbuhel, and the Stubaital *and* next-door Seefeld, where the cross-country skiing is unsurpassed in Europe. Besides having more than enough ski areas to keep all-level skiers happily schussing, culturally-rich Innsbrook is rife with sightseeing opportunities, restaurants specializing in Tyrolean dishes, and night spots. *Sample package:* $849 includes air, eight night's stay, transfers, breakfasts and dinners. A & S Travel Center, (800) 523-5279.

The Alberg Pass region is another one of Austria's most famed ski areas. It is here that ski instruction began back in 1907. The Arlberg slopes consists of five ski resorts (St. Anton, Zurs, St. Anton, St. Christoph, and Stuben) all interconnected by runs, lifts, and shuttle bus. Though they all share roughly the same snow, each one has a personality of its own and slightly different conditions. St. Anton is the most bustling of the quintet due to its easy access. Stuben, a picturesque village, is the most budget-minded resort in The Arlberg region. The highest Arlberg village, St. Christoph, is propped up in its own little world. Both Lech and Zurs are the most exclusive of the bunch, and more difficult to reach. *Sample package:* $1099 includes air, eight night's stay, transfers, breakfasts and dinners. A & S Travel Center, (800) 523-5279.

Kitzbuhel ("Kitz" for those in the know) is Austria's largest ski resort. It's also one of its loveliest Alpine villages *and*, some say, the liveliest place to be *apres-ski*. The village itself looks like a fairy tale come alive with medieval buildings that line narrow streets, and sturdy horses trot through town pulling merrymakers in shiny sleighs. The skiing is phenomenal thanks to a well-organized network of interconnected lifts for more than 20 miles of runs. It covers two separate mountains including the Hahnenkamm, for which the most famous downhill race in the world was named. *Sample package:* $1049 includes air, eight night's stay, transfers, breakfasts and dinners. A & S Travel Center, (800) 523-5279.

At all Austrian ski areas, you can count on finding a scintillating *apres-ski* life. As soon as the last run is made, skiers crowd into mountain huts to drink Jagertee (a warm tea with spices and Austrian rum) and before long, a full-fledged party—complete with singing—is going on. You can also count on finding restaurants that serve wonderful dumpling soups, wiener schnitzel, and other Austrian specialties as well as homemade pastries such as *Apfelstrudel* and *Kaiserschmarren* (a light pancake smeared with jam and sugar) and an excellent assortment of local beers and wines.

Scandinavia

A young blonde glides along silently on her cross-country skis, look-alike baby (with red nose) following on a sled of her own. A group of blue-eyed Norwegians feast on crispbread and Jarlsberg in a cluster of birch trees alongside a trail. A five-year-old dons a numbered vest, ready to compete in a cross-country race for juniors. These are not Carl Larsson paintings (though they could be), these are everyday scenes in Scandinavia during the winter months.

Cross-country—or Nordic—skiing originally was how one got around the remote wilderness areas of Scandinavia. Today, it is widely regarded as one of the best ways to be close to nature, enjoy the crystal-clear air fragrant with pine, and exercise. However, Scandinavia not only offers some of the best cross-country ski networks in the world, but is home to some respectable downhill mountains as well.

Two of the best places for North Americans to ski in Norway are its capital, Oslo and Lillehammer, which will be the site of the XVII Winter Olympics Games in 1994.

No other capital in the world has skiing as it is in Oslo. The city is ringed by an astounding 1500 miles of cross-country trails marked and maintained by the Norwegian ski association. Lillehammer is Norway's center for winter sports. Though world-renown for its cross-country trails (many of which are lit for night skiing), it also has 12 miles of downhill runs as well as all other winter sports such as ice skating and sledding. *Sample package:* (Lillehammer): $895 includes air, rail transportation to Lillehammer, five night's stay in Lillehammer hotel with breakfast and dinner daily, plus one night in Oslo with breakfast. Bennett Tours, (800) 221-2420.

In Sweden, there are over 500 ski areas. Skiing is not just a "sport" in this country, it's a passion. Nearly two-thirds of the natives cross-country, and one-third skis downhill. Two of the most popular ski areas offering both are Salen in the province of Darlarna and Are/Duved, the country's largest ski area. For those wanting to try summer skiing—under the midnight sun—the lifts all the way north in Riksgransen stay open from the middle of May until mid-summer until 1 A.M. Air/land packages are not available from the U.S. See your travel agent.

In Finland, you'll find some of the finest cross-country trail networks in the world up north in Finnish Lapland. (Pssst! You'll also find Santa's official home and workshop and can add your child's name to the mailing list for postcards from Santa). For downhill, there's world-class skiing in the southern city of Lahti, about an hour's drive from Helsinki. *Sample package* (Lapland): $756 includes air, seven night's stay, transfers. Finnair, (800) 950-5000.

In Iceland—which, incidentally, is the easiest of all the aforementioned to reach, a mere five-hour flight from New

York—you'll find both cross-country and downhill (more of the latter) near the capital city, Reykjavik and northern hub of Akureyri. *Sample package* (Reykjavik): $529 includes air, three night's stay with breakfast daily, and sightseeing trip. Icelandair, (800) 223-5500.

The Scandinavian brand of *apres-ski* is a sauna followed by an ultra-healthy meal (massive smorgasbords with a mind-boggling selection of herrings, smoked trout, salmon dishes, cheeses, cold cuts, pates, salads, warm meat and poultry dishes, vegetables, desserts, and more) and later, quiet conversation or wild dancing and partying in discotheques.

Aside from skiing in the Scandinavian countries, there's a mesmerizing variety of other winter activities including sleigh rides (pulled by reindeer), icebreaker cruises, snowmobile safaris and a packed-calendar of events (ski races, ice golf tournaments, snow sculpture competitions, and reindeer driving competitions).

CHAPTER 15

Travel Books

15.1 Guidebooks

In the past, the big travel book names such as Fodor's and Frommer's dominated the travel book market. Today, however, there are scores of independent travel book publishers such as Lonely Planet Publications, The Mountaineer Books, Sasquatch Books, Ulysses Press . . . the list goes on and on.

These guidebooks are constantly on the lookout for writers—especially writers who specialize in certain geographical areas—to author and co-author books. Not only do they need writers to initially write the books, but often require annual updating.

There are both advantages and drawbacks to writing guidebooks. Perhaps the best thing is that you can devote a chunk of time to researching one geographical area. That way, you become somewhat of an expert and can spin off a variety of magazine and newspaper articles in addition to the chapter or book. If you update the chapter or chapter every year, it becomes a check you can count on.

However, the pay is usually quite lamentable. While you may make a dollar a word writing for magazines, guidebook writing can end up paying less than a nickel a word. On top of that, most guidebook work is very time consuming since the books generally include extraordinary detail about the destinations they cover.

Since the compensation is not always very good, consider whether it's to your advantage to have such a credit. If you want to write a lot about South America for magazines and newspapers, it sure helps to be able to say that you wrote or co-authored a book on South America. If it's an first-rate publisher, it's instant credibility.

If you're co-authoring a book, find out where your name will appear. Will it be on the cover? At the beginning of each chapter? In a list of contributors? Generally, the writer has no say in the matter, but it can't hurt to ask. Try to get your name on the actual section of the book you write.

Think carefully before signing the contract. Can you ascertain the details they require in the time allotted? Can you visit each and every place you are expected to write about? Can you allow this much time for one project? Can you afford this?

15.2 Other Travel-Related Books

Once you've established yourself as a travel writer, you can begin proposing your own travel books to publishers. Your best bet is to get an agent who will do the actual selling. If you have a friend that can recommend an agent, ask if you can contact them. If not, take a look at the list of agents in *Literary Market Place* in the library. Send samples of your work and a book proposal and follow up within a month's time. Most agents get a standard fee of 15 percent of royalties on domestic sales.

CHAPTER 16

Other Travel Writing/Editing Jobs

16.1 Guidebook Editing

Many of the travel book publishers hire independent contractors—or freelance editors—to edit their annually published guidebooks. This can entail making assignments and working with writers as well as editing. If you want an occasional break from writing, editing guidebooks does offer a change. It's a good idea to contact some of the publishing houses and let them know of your interest. Here again, if you have an expertise in a geographical area or travel specialty—such as adventure travel, cruise travel, or RV travel—it helps.

16.2 Travel Promotionals

There's an enormous amount of travel information produced every year by hotels, tourism offices, tour operators, airlines—you name it. On top of that, there are all sorts of mediums for distributing the information including newsletters, brochures, and computer services (such as Prodigy and Compuserve). All of these require writers and editors. The best way to land these jobs is to zero in on three or four companies and introduce yourself to them. Of course, the more credentials you have in the specific geographical area they represent, the better.

Part Six

SELF PROMOTION

CHAPTER 17

Getting Your Name Around

17.1 Send Out Clips

Once you have a byline on a travel piece—even if it's just a featurette or a vignette—the door to travel writing can swing wide open if you want it to.

Clips of that very first article—and all subsequent articles—should be sent to anyone who helped with the trip or was mentioned in the piece. For example, if it's an article about Long Beach, California, send it to the Long Beach Convention and Visitors Bureau, the California Division of Tourism. If you mention restaurants, hotels, or airlines, send it to them. You might also send a copy of it to anyone else you met while researching it.

Always attach a note (preferably on personalized note paper that includes your name, address, and phone number) saying something along the lines of:

Dear Eileen,

I thought you might like to see my article that appeared in The Ridgefield Press.

Thanks for your assistance.

If you don't have a contact name, call and ask for the director of tourism, the hotel manager, a shopkeeper or other person in charge. Don't bother sending clips to "Whom It May Concern."

Try to send out these clips (also called tear sheets) or good xeroxes of them—as soon as they're in print. One copy is sufficient.

17.2 Attend Press Events

In order to become a successful, widely published travel writer, it's necessary to cultivate contacts all over the travel industry. Of course, there are always exceptions, but by in large, the more editors, publishers, and writers you can meet, the more chances you have of getting published. The more public relations people you meet, the more information you'll have direct access to.

If you live in a metropolitan area, your goal should be to attend at least one travel industry event a week. Many metropolitan area travel editors and writers customarily attend three or four a week—including lunches, dinners, and receptions. How do you get invited?

If you have written about a destination and sent copies to the public relations agency that represents the area, one of its hotels or another client, chances are you'll automatically be invited to press events they host.

If not, however, in the beginning, you may have to invest in the price of a lunch or dinner. Start by scanning the calendar listings in *Publishers Weekly* for information on any industry functions you might be interested in attending. For example, the American Society of Journalists and Authors (ASJA) holds monthly meetings which often include lunch or dinner and a lecture or panel discussion on anything from "How to Use Research Resources" to "How to Get Published in Magazines." The price is generally about $45 for non-members; $35 for members.

If you know any travel writers or editors that are members in the Society of American Travel Writers, New York Travel Writers, Bay Area Travel Writers or any other travel writer groups (see Appendix B), ask if you can be their guest at a monthly lunch meeting. Tell them up front that you will pay your own way—which is usually the price of the meal (roughly $25–35). With the exception of annual business meetings, most of these groups encourage guests.

Once you are in the door at any of these events, make a pact with yourself that you will meet—and exchange cards with—at least two or three other professionals. Do not walk around with a stack of cards passing them out as if fliers on a street corner. Only exchange cards when it seems entirely appropriate.

When you return home, on the individual cards jot down the date and place you met. If you talked for some time, you might consider sending them a brief note acknowledging how much you enjoyed meeting them or calling to set up a lunch date.

From there, your contacts can begin to multiply and before you know it, you'll find yourself getting "on the circuit" where invitations come in quite regularly. When you become members of any travel groups, you will automatically receive many invitations.

If you're not within easy reach of urban events, consider attending writers' workshops and conferences periodically. Before signing up, check to see if any workshops specifically on travel writing are offered. These are also an excellent way to meet editors, publishers, and writers.

17.3 Be a Joiner

Once you've published, you'll find there are several associations you might benefit from joining. Many have monthly meetings in which you can meet editors and others in the field (see Appendix B).

Make Networking Work

A hungry, pushy writer is a big turnoff. If you have managed to get yourself to an event where you have the opportunity to meet editors, publishers, and other writers, do yourself a big favor and take it easy. Many editors complain about freelance writers who are constantly trying to pitch story ideas at press events. Most editors are more attracted to the writer who is "swamped" with work. The implication is that they must be very good since they are in such demand. Even if you are desperate for work, under no circumstances let it show. Also, keep the following tips in mind.

1. *Project a very professional image*

Though writers in general have the reputation of being sloppy dressers, not all are. Many freelancers offend editors by their slovenly dressing. This does not mean you have to dress like a lawyer or a banker; a certain amount of personal style and creativity is often a reflection of how creative you are.

2. *Keep business cards handy*

If you have a pile of business cards in your jacket pocket or an easy-to-reach area of a briefcase, it saves having to awkwardly dig around for one when someone asks. Do not hold them in hand, however. That's a little too eager.

3. *Watch what you say*

Nobody likes a braggart, a name-dropper, or a conversation hog.

4. *Pay attention*

Keep your focus on the person you are talking to. At receptions, there is a big temptation to continuously look around the room to see who else is there. This can be enormously distracting and outright rude. If you find yourself talking to someone who does this—a surprising number of editor-in-chiefs and other high-on-the-masthead editors do this—move on as soon as possible. You are wasting your time talking to someone who is probably not listening.

5. *Don't pour your heart out*

Every now and then—whether at a press party or on a press trip—you'll have the unfortunate experience of meeting someone who spills out his/her guts about a current affair in their life. That doesn't mean you are obligated to tell your story. If a person is distraught enough—or intoxicated—to talk about it to a near-stranger, they are probably telling taxi drivers all over town. The net result will inevitably be embarrassment on their part. By sharing your own experience, you will get yourself in even deeper.

6. *Take an interest in them personally*

Small talk can be excruciatingly boring, especially if it goes on for long. If you find yourself talking to someone for long, change the subject. Ask them where how they became a travel writer or where they are from originally. This can often lead to wonderful small-world stories.

17.4 Cultivate Friendships within the Industry

Though it's all very cliché, very often a particular travel writer will get an assignment not necessarily because they are the best person in the world to write the piece, but because they happen to be in the right place at the right time.

If you know a lot of people in the business and you're a good writer, chances are good that your name will come up in editorial meetings. To insure that it does, it's necessary to keep your name—your byline—on people's mind. If you spend a lot of your socializing time with various people within the industry, you will be on their minds.

Chances are, you will naturally gravitate to writers and editors anyway, since you have so much in common. Make a point of getting to know them over time. If you have tickets to the theater, invite an editor. Suggest meeting for lunch. Set up a game of tennis. You might also consider throwing small parties and inviting editors and writers you know to celebrate a move, a new contract, or a holiday.

17.5 Send Out Press Releases

There are a handful of public relations newsletters and various other newsletters that print writers' editorial needs for free. The advantage of this is that it's an opportunity to get your name out there in circulation as well as alert those who can help you as to what you need. The disadvantage is that you may get a lot of mail and phone calls when you're too busy to deal with them (see Appendix A for a list of newsletters).

Get in the habit of sending a monthly announcement to the various newsletters regarding your editorial needs. Be sure to print it on your letterhead and keep the information brief and to the point. It might read something like this:

> For release: October 7, 1992
>
> Travel Writer Ann Denneaux needs information on historic inns in New England for an article currently in the works. In addition, she welcomes any news on Caribbean restaurants and hotels for a book she is updating. Please feel free to send press materials to her at 322 West 104th Street, New York, NY 10025. No phone calls please.

You might also send announcements to various newsletters and publications alerting the industry of any geographical or professional move you make.

> Ann Denneaux has recently left her position as travel editor of *Country Bride* magazine to become a freelance writer. She is continu-

ing to cover the honeymoon travel market and welcomes information. Please feel free to send press materials to her at 322 West 104th Street, New York, NY 10025.

or

Travel writer Ann Denneaux is pleased to announce that she has moved. All future mailings should be sent to her at 322 West 104th Street, New York, NY 10025. Her new phone number is 212-000-0000. A fax number is available on request only.

17.6 Author's Biographies and Press Kits

Whenever a publisher or editor is looking for a writer, they'll often ask to see either a résumé or an author's biography. It's a good idea to have a "bio" in your computer which you can print out and send around whenever anyone asks for a copy. It should include a bit about your background (including educational and professional), the publications you've been published in, any books you've written, any awards you've won, and any professional organizations you may belong to.

For example:

About the Author

Up until the end of 1988, Susan Farewell was one of the travel editors of Conde Nast's *Bride's* magazine in New York City. For nine years, she combed the globe looking for honeymoon destinations.

Ms. Farewell left Conde Nast to become a freelance writer and editor and now contributes (travel pieces, book reviews, and general interest articles) to such magazines as *Vogue España* (published in Madrid), *Travel and Leisure*, *Metropolitan Home*, *Child*, *Bridal Guide*, *Gulliver* (published in Tokyo), *Diversion*, *Discovery* (including one cover story), and *Caribbean Travel and Life.* Her work also appears in newspapers such as *Crain's New York Business*, *Crain's Chicago Business*, *The New York Post*, and *St. Petersburg Times.*

In addition, she is the author of the best-selling *Mobil Road Atlas and Trip Planning Guide* (published annually), the *New England Atlas*, and the *Pacific Northwest Atlas*, all published by Simon & Schuster. Her most recent book *How to Make a Living as a Travel Writer* was published by Paragon House in 1992.

In *The Independent Traveler*, a newsletter published quarterly by Prentice Hall Travel division, Susan has a column called "Trips, Tips, and Travel Hits." It is distributed to bookstores around the country.

She has co-authored several books including *The Penguin Guide to New York City*, *The Penguin Guide to the Caribbean*, Fodor's *Selected Resorts and Hotels of the U.S.*, and *Hidden Guide to New England* (Ulysses Press).

Susan is a member of the New York Travel Writers and the Society of American Travel Writers, and periodically lectures on travel writing and photography. She studied Greek Classics at Boston University and in Athens, Greece and now lives in South Salem, New York.

Ideally, you should have a press kit made up. Customarily, these are pocketed folders filled with professional information about you, the writer. Contents generally include:

An author's biography
A large black and white photograph
Sample articles
Book reviews on any books you may have written
Articles that have been written about you
A list of your areas of expertise

Part Seven

MONEY MATTERS

CHAPTER
18

Earnings

18.1 What You Can Expect to Make

You can take all sorts of time to figure out what your *per diem* rate would be, but as a travel writer, you are more often than not paid what they—the newspapers, the magazines, the book publishers—pay, rather than what you charge. And what they pay varies greatly. You could very easily write a 1000-word article for a magazine and make $1000, or sell it to a newspaper for $200. If the same article appeared in a book, it may ultimately bring in just $50.

For those figures, you'd have to write a lot of articles to make any money. Even if you sold one $1000 piece a month, you'd only make $12,000 a year. Hardly a living.

In order to make a substantial living—anywhere from $35,000–$85,000 a year (or more), it's best to have at least one major annual project that brings in a chunk of money along with a variety of other projects. Here's what you should strive for:

1. *Land a corporate client*

Easier said than done, you are most likely thinking. However, these clients do exist. Just look in your mail. Many of the credit card companies send out travel newsletters. Airlines send out newsletters. Some of the oil and insurance companies have their own magazines and book divisions. Prodigy has a newsletter. These are regular publications that need crackerjack travel writers and editors. Do some research. Send your credentials to the travel department managers. These can be very lucrative projects with annual contracts.

2. *Get yourself a column*

Another easier-said-than-done suggestion. However, these can be found or invented. Start with a lesser-known publication such as a regional magazine or weekly newspaper. Though you may make only a couple hundred dollars a month writing it, it's a wonderful credit to have and once you've piled up a stack of columns, you can sell yourself to a bigger, better paying consumer magazine.

3. *Spin-off articles*

If you spend a month traveling around the Pacific Northwest to research a guidebook, try to pitch several story angles to a variety of magazines and newspapers on that area. Get as many assignments out of one trip as possible.

4. *Recycle, reslant, rewrite, resell your work*

Unless you've sold all rights or signed a "work for hire" contract, you may be able to make more money from your articles. Generally, American magazines buy first North American rights only, which means you are free to turn around and sell the same article to another publication at another time (be sure to check your contract for specifics). You could simultaneously sell the same article to a North American magazine and a foreign magazine. Save everything you write, you may be able to use bits and pieces of articles in subsequent articles or books.

5. *Specialize*

Consider specializing on a geographical area or a travel specialty that is in demand. You don't necessarily have to commit to this for life, but it can help for stretches of your career. For example, some writers specialize in the Caribbean, the Far East, or Europe. Some specialize in honeymoon travel, business travel, adventure travel, cruise travel, eco-tourism—you name it.

6. *Write advertorials*

Mention you're writing an advertorial to an editor and they may look down their nose at you. Some writers will as well, except those who have made a chunk of money writing advertorials themselves. For some, writing advertorials is the same as writing ad copy—hardly journalism. However, the reality is that many travel advertorials are not at all different from editorials. The difference however, can be money. Advertorials usually pay between $1 and $4 a word.

7. *Write brochures and other promotional travel pieces*

This—like the advertorials—can be tricky, however. It's important to separate the journalist you from the promotional you. If you write brochures for Hilton Hotels and then try to sell an unbiased piece about "The World's Best International Hotels," your credibility is seriously at question.

8. *Take on editing jobs*

If you consider yourself an editor as well as a writer, sell yourself as such.

18.2 What to Negotiate For

Budgets vary from publishing house to publishing house, but it can't hurt to ask for the following, once you get established.

1. *More money*

Widely published, big-name travel writers can often name their price. The average professional travel writer, on the other hand, usually must accept what's offered. Still, occasionally you can squeeze a little bit more money out of their budget.

2. *Travel expenses*

Some publications pay for travel expenses, others don't. If they don't, confirm beforehand whether they accept articles written from subsidized trips and have them send you an assignment letter. If they do, keep a meticulous record—along with all receipts—while on the road.

3. *Telephone and mailing expenses*

Many travel pieces require making multiple long-distance calls and doing major mailings. Ask to be reimbursed for all. They can say yes or no, or cover some of the expenses.

4. *Deadlines*

Ask for more time right at the outset if you think you're going to need it. Editors almost always give writers phony deadlines. This way, you might also have time to work on other assignments during the same period.

5. *A byline*

Always ask if your name will be on the piece, even if it's a publication that does not necessarily include bylines.

18.3 When You Can Expect to be Paid

For most magazines articles, you will be paid not much sooner than six weeks after you submit your article. Some do not pay until the piece actually runs.

Most newspapers pay only after the article appears.

Travel book publishers customarily pay one-half against royalties upon the signing of the contract, and the other half upon acceptance of the completed manuscript.

CHAPTER 19

Record Keeping

19.1 Find a Good Accountant

It's very important to find an accountant who works for self-employed people, better yet, if he/she works with writers. If they understand the travel writing business, all the better. And do yourself a big favor, don't wait until tax time. Make an appointment with an accountant right when you go into business for yourself.

Once he/she helps you set up a good bookkeeping system, you'll most likely need their services only once a year at tax time.

19.2 Set Up a Bookkeeping System

If you keep good records throughout the year, you will not have to take time out from writing every spring to do your taxes. Consider keeping the following records:

1. *A day book*

In this book, write down how much you spend on business expenses each day. For example:

October 5th, 1992

$ 6.00	Train from Bedford to New York City.
$60.00	Lunch with editor (give name, title, publication, and reason for lunch)
$ 8.50	Travel magazines for research
$ 5.50	Taxi to editorial meeting (give publication name, editors name, and reason for meeting)
$ 6.00	Taxi from meeting to train station
$ 6.00	Train from New York City to Bedford
$92.00	Total

2. *Monthly receipt envelopes*

Keep all receipts and make sure they are dated. On each one, jot down what it was for. Have one envelope (6″ by 9″ is a good size)—or a collapsible folding envelope which is divided by months—for each month of the year. Each day, put all new receipts in the envelope.

3. *A motor vehicle mileage log*

This should be kept in the automobile you use for business. You can buy one in a paper goods store or just jot the information down in a little notebook. Every time you use the vehicle for business, register the date, the destination, the business purpose, and the mileage reading at the beginning and at the end of the trip. If an assistant or somebody else working for you uses the car, his or her name should be recorded as well. At the end of each month, add up how many miles you used the car for business.

4. *A binder filled with columnar pages*

Divide the binder into at least two sections. One for expenses, the other for billing information. If you have other categories—

such as independent contractors—you'll need a section for those as well.

For business expenses At the end of each month, add up monthly totals (from day book) spent on rent, meals, transportation, research materials, and all other business expenses and put them in the appropriate columns. Write in pencil, round out numbers.

Here's a sample:

	Rent	*Electricity*	*Telephone*	*Express Mail*
January	1000.	65.	153.	42.
February	1000.	66.	210.	0.
March	1000.	58.	155.	12.
April	1000.	50.	141.	6.
1st quarter totals:	4000.	239.	659.	60.

Use as many sheets as necessary and include other categories such as office insurance, automobile expenses, public transportation, meals (research or entertainment), membership dues, admission fees, accountant's fee, messengers, U.S. postage, periodicals, copying charges, research books, classes, and workshops. Break down all travel expenses as well—airfare, accommodations, airport transfers, tips, meals, taxis, car rental, etc.

For billing information, divide the columns as follows, using one sheet for each quarter. This serves as a record of how much you earn:

First Quarter Invoices
1992

Date	*Invoice Number*	*Company or Publication*	*Contact*	*Subject*	*Fee*	*Date Received*
1/03	205	Wanderings	S. Lewis	Inns	$2000.	2/12
1/08	206	Top Books	H. Wood	Maine	$3000.	2/20

Use a separate sheet for reimbursable expenses with the same format as the invoice record.

If you hire anyone to work for you, be sure to keep a record of what you pay. For example:

Independent Contractors

Date Amount	*Name*	*Social Security #*	*Check Date*	*Check #*
1/15 $300.	A. Lien	133-44-0000	1/15	1049

If you pay any one independent contractor over $600 in one tax year, it is necessary to send out a special tax form in January of the following year. This is something your accountant can do if you provide him/her with their name, address, telephone and social security number, along with the total amount you paid them.

5. *A folder for copies of invoices*

For every invoice you send out, keep a hard copy for yourself in a file folder.

6. *A folder for independent contractors*

For all invoices you receive from freelancers who work for you, keep their original invoice and write on it the amount you paid, the date, and the check number.

19.3 Tax Deductions

As a self-employed travel writer who probably works out of your home, you'll find deductions practically with every step you take. That is, of course, if you are writing travel pieces for a living. For maximum tax deductions, it's important to sit down with an accountant who keeps abreast of the changing tax laws.

19.4 Paying Taxes

Depending on which state you live in, you are required to pay federal and state or city taxes in four installments throughout the year. These quarterly estimates are due on April 15, June 15, September 15, and January 15 or the Monday that follows those dates if they fall on Sundays. It helps to write a reminder on your calendar a week or so before each payment is due, so you don't forget. Your accountant can provide you with the government vouchers that should accompany payment.

19.5 Invoices

Every time you complete an article or any other project, you should automatically send out an invoice. Begin by numbering your very first one #100 and subsequent ones 101, 102, 103, etc. Here's a sample of what to include:

INVOICE 150

Date:	October 8, 1992
Attention:	Editor's Name Editor's Exact Title Publication Street address City, State, and Zip
Subject:	"New England Inns" article for March 1993 issue.
Amount Due:	$1000.
Payment Due:	Your Name Street Address City, State, and Zip
Social Security:	Your social security number

CHAPTER
20

Assurances and Insurances

20.1 Emergency Funds

As a freelancer, you will find there are times when you have three and four checks arriving in the same week. You will also find that there are times when checks don't show up for months. There are also good years where you're constantly busy, and bad years where you are not making any money. Before launching your travel writing business, it's imperative that you have an emergency savings account. Ideally, the amount should be enough to pay all your expenses for six months to a year. Each year, add at least 3 percent of your salary. The money should be kept in something liquid like a money market or CD rather than locked away. It should not be touched unless absolutely necessary.

20.2 Disability Insurance

In the unfortunate event you become disabled and cannot work beyond the period your emergency fund covers, you could have a serious problem at hand if you don't have disability insurance. This is an absolute must for self-employed writers. When choosing a coverage, get the broadest policy you can and make sure you are covered for doing the job you do. With disability insurance, there is an elimination period which generally means you are paid after 60 or 90 days of becoming disabled or you can opt to be paid immediately. If you have an emergency fund, you can opt for the elimination period in order to reduce the monthly cost of the coverage.

20.3 Keogh Retirement Plans

A Keogh retirement plan is an excellent way to reduce your taxable income as well as save for your future. Each year, you can put away as much as 25 percent (or $30,000, whichever is less) of your self-employment income and deduct that amount on your tax return. You don't have to pay taxes on the amount until you begin withdrawals, which, presumably, will be after you retire.

The annual deadline for making contributions to Keogh plans is your tax-filing deadline which for most people is April 15th. To initially open it, however, the plan must be established by December 31st of the year for which you plan to take deductions. At that point, you are required to deposit a minimum of $750.

In order to insure that you have the cash to make an annual contribution to your Keogh, consider saving a set amount every month.

Part Eight

YOUR HOME OFFICE

CHAPTER 21

Setting Up

21.1 The Space

Walk into any travel writer's home and even though their "office" may be behind a shut door, there are piles of papers and books in the living room, in the dining room, sometimes even the bathroom. Few travel writers can physically—and mentally—divide work and living space.

Still, the actual office should be at least one room reserved exclusively for your work, for both tax and sanity reasons. The amount of space you need will depend on how efficient a filer and how much of a pack rat you are. The travel industry generates an extraordinary amount of paperwork, so the more room you have the better.

The main thing is that you feel comfortable in your office. It shouldn't be noisy. It shouldn't be stuffy and stifling. Your chair should be ergonomically safe and comfortable. Lighting should be very good.

Of course, if you are lucky enough to live in a place that has a beautiful, inspiring view—all the better.

When figuring out how much room you will need, take the following into consideration. You will need:

1. Space for a desk and chair. Even better is to have two desks—one for your computer and printer, the other for

writing out bills, recording notes from telephone interviews, and general bookkeeping.

2. Storage space for filing cabinets. Many travel writers divide filing cabinets by destinations. For example, every time you receive a press release about Greece, you simply slip it into the "Greece" folder. You will also need to file multiple copies of your articles.
3. Bookshelves for guidebooks, travel books, and reference books.
4. Shelf space or drawer space for supplies.
5. Storage space for filing slides, maps, illustrations, and any other illustrative material.

21.2 The Equipment

When you first start out as a travel writer, you will have to invest in certain pieces of office equipment to set up a home office, but once you get settled, there are very few operating expenses. And though you may pride yourself on the fact that you do your best work on an antique manual typewriter at your kitchen table, you will have to become high-tech if you want to survive in the competitive travel writing business. In fact the higher, the better. Consider the consequences: if two writers are just as qualified for an assignment and one is able to send in their manuscript by modem, as opposed to the other who would send in a hard copy that would have to scanned or keyboarded into the publication's system, as an editor—who would you give the assignment to?

Make it your business to keep on top of technology available to writers. To save space, consider getting integrated equipment, such as a computer equipped with a fax, or a combination copier/fax machine. To save headaches, consider buying proven brand-name equipment. Though you can function on less, ultimately your office should have the following pieces of equipment.

1. *A computer system with printer*

Whether to go with an IBM-compatible or a Macintosh is the biggest question. Before kerplunking down the credit card, take a poll. Do the editors you know use an IBM? What do other writers use? Whatever you choose, make sure it has enough memory to run several programs at once and a hard disk drive that can store large programs (usually 40 Mb or more). Try to get a printer which prints letter-quality documents.

Many travel writers own laptops on which they do all their work—at home and on the road. Others are perfectly happy with word processors.

2. *Word processing and other software*

When deciding which word processing program to buy, this is another time to take a poll. Many travel writers swear by WordPerfect. There are several other writer programs including dictionaries, grammar checkers, and plot planners. In addition, consider getting a database system (for mailing lists), and a spreadsheet program (for managing your financial records), or an integrated package which combines word processing, database, and spreadsheet programs. If you plan to create newsletters, brochures, or other professional documents, you'll need desktop publishing software.

3. *A 2400-baud modem*

You will inevitably have opportunities to send and receive computer files via modem. In addition to the modem, you'll need communications software.

4. *A fax machine*

Even if you don't mind running down to the local printers to send out and receive an occasional fax, it's worth investing in your own fax machine. More and more editors, publishers, and industry personnel are relying on transmitting documents by fax. Though you can get a reliably good fax machine for about $500, consider investing in a plain-paper machine. Though considerably more expensive (at press time, the cheapest was about $2000), they use regular copy paper which is better than the slippery thermal paper that eventually darkens. Also, some of them double as copier machines, which saves you from having to buy a copy machine.

5. *Two phone lines*

Though call-waiting is a convenient telephone feature, it can be very disruptive to conducting business. For example, if you keep being interrupted in the middle of an interview, you may irritate the person you are interviewing. If you have your fax and modem sharing the same line, call waiting can also botch up electronic transmissions.

Your best bet is to have one line as your main business number and a second line for other calls, the fax machine, and modem. When not using the latter, keep the second line free and arrange with the telephone company for the "hunt" feature. With this feature, if the caller dials the first number and you are using it, the call automatically jumps to the second line. That way, if you are in the middle of an important conversation on phone line number one, you can simply put an answering machine on the second line and let it pick up your calls. The second line can also serve as your personal phone number.

6. *An answering machine for both phone lines*

Fax Cover Sheets

To look really professional, make up a standard fax form on your computer and run off several copies on letterhead. Each time you send one, fill in the specific details in pen. Here's an example:

FAX FAX FAX

Attention: ______________________________

Company: ______________________________

Fax Number: ______________________________

Date: ______________________________

From: ______________________________

Fax Number: ______________________________

Number of Pages (including Cover Sheet): ______________

Message: ______________________________

____

____

____

____

7. *A desktop copier*

If you have to drive half an hour or walk six blocks and then spend 25 cents every time you need to make a copy of something, you're probably better off investing in your own machine.

A Word About Service Contracts

When you purchase your computer, your printer, your fax machine, and any other electronic machinery, you will generally be asked whether you want a service contract that will go into effect after the warranty runs out. These generally cover repair service and parts if any breakdowns occur. If you have the cash available, it's always a good idea. If cash is limited at the time, consider getting service contracts only for equipment that is high risk. What's high risk? Anything with movable parts, such as a printer and a fax machine.

21.3 Paperwork

Before ordering business cards, letterhead, and other stationery goods for your business, take time to think about the image you want to project. One of the most enjoyable things about being in business for yourself is that you don't have to conform. You don't have to have a conventional white card with black lettering. You can be as creative as you want. Look at other people's cards and letterhead. What do you like about it? Is their name big? Is the card a different shape? Is the color scheme attractive? Chances are, your name is the name of your company. It's your byline, your company logo. It's a label, like Ralph Lauren or Calvin Klein. Show it off the best you can, without being pretentious.

It's a good idea to include your title along with your name, address and phone number, though some writers prefer not to. The title can be as you like it: Travel Writer, Editor/Writer, Travel Journalist, Journalist, Scribe, Reporter. Avoid listing the associations you belong to on letterhead and business cards. A good name doesn't need endorsements.

Unless you don't mind getting all sorts of unsolicited fax junk mail, instead of including your fax number, have the card and letterhead say, "Fax available on request." In fact, do yourself a big favor and never list your fax number on membership rosters or any other place.

In addition to business cards, letterhead, and matching envelopes, consider ordering small pads of paper that have your name, address, and phone numbers on them. These can easily be clipped to copies of your articles and sent to various people.

APPENDIX A

Travel Writers' Resources

Your Office Library

A travel writer's library should include a good desk-size dictionary, a French/English dictionary, a world atlas, and a North American road atlas along with the following titles:

A Writer's Guide to Copyright, New York: Poets & Writers, 1990. A summary of copyright law.

Bunnin, Brad, and Beren, Peter, *The Writer's Legal Companion*, Reading, Mass.: Addison-Wesley, 1988. A guide to contracts, taxes, agent relationships and more.

The Chicago Manual of Style, Chicago: The University of Chicago Press, 1982. For any grammatical questions that come up.

The New York Public Library Desk Reference, New York: Simon & Schuster, 1989. A tremendous source of information.

Rodale, J. I., *The Synonym Finder*, New York: Warner, 1978. An excellent thesaurus.

Strunk, William Jr., and White, E. B., *The Elements of Style*, New York: Macmillan, 1979. A must for all writers.

Travel Industry Personnel Directory, New York: Fairchild Publications (published annually). This lists airlines, shiplines, railroads, car rental agencies, tour operators, tourist offices, travel organizations, and hotel representatives.

Writer's Market, Cincinnati, Ohio: Writer's Digest Books, published annually. Lists most of the nation's book and magazine publishers along with information on contests, agents, and syndicates.

The Public Library

You'll most likely find yourself in the public library often researching travel articles. Do familiarize yourself with the following two publications:

Encyclopedia of Associations, Detroit: Gale Research, updated periodically. This list thousands of associations you may need to contact for research.

Literary Market Place, New York: Bowker, published annually. A complete listing of all national book and magazine publishing sources, agents, and other industry personnel.

Useful Subscriptions

Consumer Reports Travel Letter (Box 53629, Boulder, CO 80322–3629) A monthly offshoot from *Consumer Reports* magazine filled with inside travel information.

Poets & Writers (72 Spring Street, New York, NY 10012). Published six times a year. Includes author interviews, resources list, and information about various grants and awards available.

Publishers Weekly, (249 West 17 Street, New York, NY 10011). A weekly magazine highlighting news in the book publishing world.

Travelwriter Marketletter (The Waldorf Astoria, 301 Park Avenue, #1850, New York, NY 10022) lists new markets, editorial staff changes, information on writer's workshops, and other useful information every month.

Publicity Opportunities

The following newsletters list editorial needs of editors and writers:

Contacts, CAP Communications, 35–20 Broadway, Astoria, NY 11106; (718) 721–0508.

Jack O'Dwyer's Newsletter, 271 Madison Avenue, New York, NY 10016; (212) 679–2471.

Partyline, 35 Sutton Place, New York, NY 10022; (212) 755–3487.

Travel Publicity Leads, McKenzie Communications, 56 South Whitney Street, Amherst, MA 01002; (413) 256–6480.

APPENDIX B

Writers' Associations

THERE are quite a few advantages to joining a writers' association. They're usually great for networking. Many have monthly meetings, some have workshops and seminars, some have annual conferences. Most have some sort of newsletter which has valuable tips and inside information. With some, you can get medical and dental plans. Some have awards activities, a membership roster.

Some have very demanding requirements for membership, others you just can write a check for. There is usually an application fee, an initiation fee, and annual dues. Here is a partial listing.

AMERICAN SOCIETY OF JOURNALISTS
AND AUTHORS, INC. (ASJA)
1501 Broadway, Suite 1907
New York, NY 10036
(212) 997–0947

ASSOCIATION FOR AUTHORS (AFA)
4189 Bellaire Boulevard, Suite 222
Houston, TX 77025
(713) 666–9711

AUTHOR'S GUILD (AG)
234 West 44th Street
New York, NY 10036
(212) 398–0838

EDITORIAL FREELANCERS' ASSOCIATION (EFA)
P.O. Box 2050, Madison Square Station
New York, NY 10159
(212) 677–3357

FLORIDA FREELANCERS ASSOCIATION (FFA)
P.O. Box 9844
Fort Lauderdale, FL 33310
(305) 485–0795

INDEPENDENT WRITERS OF CHICAGO (IWC)
7855 Grosspoint Road, #G-4
Skokie, IL 60077
(312) 676–3784

INDEPENDENT WRITERS OF SOUTHERN CALIFORNIA (IWSC)
P.O. Box 19745
Los Angeles, CA 90019
(213) 731–2652

INTERNATIONAL FOOD, WINE, AND TRAVEL WRITERS ASSOCIATION
P.O. Box 1532
Palm Springs, CA 92236–1532
(619) 346–2777

MIDWEST TRAVEL WRITERS (MTW)
420 Brickyard Road
Marquette, MI 49855
(906) 226–6007

NATIONAL WRITERS' UNION (NWU)
13 Astor Place, 17th Floor
New York, NY 10003
(212) 254–0279

NEW MEXICO OUTDOOR WRITERS
AND PHOTOGRAPHERS ASSOCIATION (NMOWPA)
P.O. Box 193
Datil, NM 87821
(505) 772–5578

PHILADELPHIA WRITERS' ORGANIZATION (PWO)
P.O. Box 42497
Philadelphia, PA 19101
(215) 387–4950

ROCKY MOUNTAIN OUTDOOR WRITERS
AND PHOTOGRAPHERS ASSOCIATION (RMOWPA)
P.O. Box 992
Tularosa, NM 88352
(505) 585–2858

ST. LOUIS WRITERS' GUILD (SLWG)
P.O. Box 7245
St. Louis, MO 63177
(314) 997–3057

SOCIETY OF AMERICAN TRAVEL WRITERS (SATW)
1155 Connecticut Avenue, NW #500
Washington, D.C. 20036
(202) 429–6639

SOCIETY OF ENVIRONMENTAL JOURNALISTS
1090 Vermont Avenue NW, Suite 1000
Washington, D.C. 20005
(215) 854–2438

SOUTHWEST WRITERS' ASSOCIATION (SWA)
P.O. Box 14632
Albuquerque, NM 87191
(505) 268–7344

TRAVEL JOURNALISTS GUILD (TJG)
P.O. Box 10643
Chicago, IL 60610
(312) 664–9279

U.S. SKI WRITERS' ASSOCIATION (USSWA)
939 Bloomfield
Hoboken, NJ 07030
(201) 656–4488

WASHINGTON INDEPENDENT WRITERS (WIW)
220 Woodward Building, 733 15th NW
Washington, D.C. 20005
(202) 347–4973

WESTERN WRITERS OF AMERICA (WWA)
1753 Victoria
Sheridan, WY 82801
(307) 672–2079

WOMEN IN COMMUNICATIONS (WIC)
3724 Executive Center Drive #165
Austin, TX 78731
(512) 346–9875

WRITERS' GUILD OF AMERICA (WGA)
555 West 57th Street
New York, NY 10019
(212) 245–6180

About the Author

SUSAN FAREWELL, an internationally published journalist, editor, and author, began traveling before she could walk and began writing about it as soon as she could put pencil to paper.

For nearly a decade, she was on the staff of Conde Nast's *Bride's* magazine, covering the honeymoon travel market. Today she writes for numerous national and foreign magazines and newspapers in addition to co-authoring and writing her own travel books.

Ms. Farewell studied Greek and Latin Classics at Boston University and at College Year in Athens, Inc., an independent study-abroad school in Athens, Greece. She is a member of the Society of American Travel Writers and The New York Travel Writers. She lives in South Salem, New York.